preserves
& pickles

preserves
& pickles

simple recipes for delicious food every day

RYLAND PETERS & SMALL
LONDON • NEW YORK

Designer Ian Midson

Production Manager Gary Hayes

Art Director Leslie Harrington

Editorial Director Julia Charles

Indexer Hilary Bird

First published in 2013
by Ryland Peters & Small
20–21 Jockey's Fields
London WC1R 4BW
and
519 Broadway, 5th Floor
New York NY 10012

www.rylandpeters.com

Text © Linda Collister, Kay Fairfax,
Liz Franklin, Tonia George, Brian
Glover, Gloria Nicol, Annie Rigg, Fiona
Smith, Laura Washburn, Lindy Wildsmith
and Ryland Peters & Small 2013

Design and photographs © Ryland
Peters & Small 2013

ISBN: 978-1-84975-449-1

10 9 8 7 6 5 4 3 2 1

A CIP record for this book is available
from the British Library.

US Library of Congress Cataloging-in-
Publication data has been applied for.

Printed and bound in China

notes:

• All spoon measurements are level, unless otherwise specified.

• All fruit and vegetables should be washed thoroughly before use in these recipes. When using citrus fruits, try to find organic or unwaxed fruits and wash well before using. If you can only find treated fruit, scrub well in warm soapy water and rinse before using.

• All eggs used in the recipes in this book are medium UK/large US, unless otherwise specified. Recipes containing raw or partially cooked egg should not be served to the very young, very old, anyone with a compromised immune system or pregnant women.

contents

Jam-making basics

Making your own pickles and preserves is a traditional part of homemaking that celebrates the seasons and somehow makes life more comforting and enjoyable. In this section you'll find out all you need to know to make the recipes in this book and more.

Choosing your ingredients

There is something so satisfying about opening a food cabinet or pantry to find the shelves stacked with colourful jars of homemade preserves. In the current climate of concerns about avoiding waste, clocking up fewer food miles, and eating seasonal, locally grown food, making preserves has never been so popular.

Where to find and buy ingredients

Nothing beats the flavour of homegrown fruit that has ripened in the sun and been picked only moments before. Using your own homegrown produce for preserving is hard to beat, because the ingredients will be fresh and you will have control over their growing conditions. Alternatively, if you know someone who grows more fruit than they can use, offer to take it off their hands in exchange for a jar of preserve that you have made from it.

Farmers' markets are another great source of fruit for preserves. You'll know that the fruit and vegetables have been grown locally, and you are more likely to find unusual varieties. Whatever its source, rinse the produce before use – although ideally not soft/bush fruits, since rinsing can reduce their juice content. However, if there is a chance they may have been sprayed, you will need to rinse and drain them.

Woodlands and hedgerows (if you live in a place where these are common) are also full of edible fruits and berries if you know what to look for. You may be lucky enough to find crab apples growing wild, along with damsons, greengages, or blackberries.

Fruit and pectin

For almost all fruit preserves you need to choose fresh, good-quality, just-ripe fruit in order to achieve the correct pectin content. This is because jam needs the right balance of pectin, acid and sugar to set properly. Different fruits contain varying amounts of pectin, and the pectin content is higher in just-ripe fruit. Fruits high in pectin include crab apples, Seville oranges, damsons, gooseberries, quinces and currants. Fruits low in pectin include strawberries, pears, elderberries, fresh apricots and cherries. Some fruits contain very little pectin, and so jams made using these fruits will need additional help to make them set. Overripe fruit can also lower the pectin content, which is why such fruit is not suitable for jams.

The pectin content can be raised in various ways. In mixed-fruit jams, the higher pectin content of one fruit can offset the lower content of another; lemon juice can be added at a rate of the juice of 1–2 lemons to every 2 kg/4 lbs. of fruit; and bottled pectin and/or special preserving sugar with added pectin can be used.

Preserving equipment

The principle underlying all preserving is to prevent decay caused by the growth of yeasts, moulds and bacteria. These organisms are destroyed when heated to sufficiently high temperatures to sterilize them, and, once sterilized, preserves must be kept securely sealed so air cannot enter. Preserves containing 60 per cent or more sugar are less susceptible to the growth of yeasts, so jams containing less sugar must be eaten more quickly.

Jars

Jars with screw-top lids are best for jams and jellies, while those with metal clip tops and rubber seals are best for chutneys and pickles. Mason jars are normally used in the United States – they have a screw-on lid consisting of two or more sections to help ensure a tight seal. European-style canning jars, which have glass tops, secured by a thick wire clamp, are also available.

You can use recycled jam or other condiment jars. Make sure they have no chips or cracks and that the lids fit well. Corrosive materials must not come into contact with the preserve, especially if it contains vinegar (as in chutneys and pickles), so be sure the lids will not corrode.

Jars must be sterilized before use. Wash the jars in hot soapy water, rinse in hot water and leave to air-dry. Place a folded dish towel on an oven shelf and lay the jars on their sides on top. Shortly before you need them, heat the oven to 110°C (225°F) Gas ¼, and leave the jars at this temperature for 20–30 minutes. The jars should still be hot when you fill them with the hot jam. Always prepare a few extra jars in case they are needed.

Other special equipment

There are a few other items you can buy for preserving:
Preserving pan A non-corrosive, non-reactive preserving pan, big enough to hold large quantities of boiling jam, is a great investment. This type of pan, sometimes known as a maslin pan or a jam pan, is wide and shallow to encourage rapid evaporation when bringing jam to setting point. A good-quality pan will have a thick, heavy base, which will prevent any preserve from burning. While copper and aluminum pans are both popular, stainless steel is best, and it is certainly necessary when making preserves that contain vinegar.

When jam is brought to a rolling boil, it rises up, so never overfill the pan. If the pan is too small and

overfilled, either you will end up with an overflowing mess of boiling syrupy jam or, in order to prevent this from happening, you won't be able to raise the temperature high enough to reach setting point.

Double boiler Useful when making fruit curds and fruit syrups and nectars, but it can be replaced by a bowl set over a pan of simmering water.

Food mill A good-quality food mill with several discs of various degrees of coarseness can be used to sieve fruit to extract a purée, which is excellent for making jams and gives a smoother texture. You can also purée apples without having to peel and core them first.

Jar funnel This is essential for pouring hot jam safely into jars. Choose one small enough to fit into most of your jars but wide enough not to become clogged with pieces of fruit. Sterilize and warm the funnel in the oven along with the jars. A sterilized, warmed scoop is useful for ladling jam into the funnel.

Jar lifter Special tongs, called a jar lifter, are used for handling the hot jars.

Jam thermometer Although not essential, this is useful for testing for setting point. Choose one that goes up to at least 110°C (230°F) and has a clip to attach it to the side of the pan.

Jelly bag A ready-made jelly bag in a plastic stand that fits over a bowl is ideal for straining juices from cooked fruit, but you can make your own from fine muslin/cheesecloth, nylon, a clean dish towel, or unbleached muslin/calico tied across the upturned legs of a stool.

Muslin/cheesecloth You will need squares of thin muslin/cheesecloth to hold seeds and spices that require cooking in with jams and chutneys. Gather the ingredients together on a generous square of fabric and tie into a bag with natural string or twine. Alternatively, buy drawstring bags made specifically for this purpose.

Waxed discs and paraffin wax Once poured into jars, hot jam should be sealed in some way. With mason jars, the seal forms part of the lid, but jars with ordinary lids require extra treatment. In Britain, waxed discs that fit 450-g/1 lb. and 900-g/2-lb. jars are available. Place the discs waxed side down on the preserve immediately after bottling before the screw-top lids are put on. Waxed discs often come with cellophane circles, which can be used as lids for jars that do not already have lids. In the United States, a layer of paraffin wax is preferred; this is readily available where canning supplies are sold. Follow the manufacturer's instructions for melting and pouring the paraffin.

Labels Label all your preserves so you know how long they have been stored. Chutneys and pickles, which benefit from a maturing period, also need to be labelled with this information.

Preserving techniques

There are two basic methods for making jam – the traditional method and the macerating method. The macerating method intensifies the flavours and will give a softer-setting jam with a more syrupy consistency.

Jam: the traditional method

The traditional method involves cooking the fruit before adding the sugar and boiling to setting point.

Cooking the fruit Place the fruit in a preserving pan with some water, the quantity of which will vary with the type of fruit you are using. Soft/bush fruits may not need any water, as they will quickly break up and release their juices when heated and mashed with a spoon. Harder fruits, however, will definitely need some water and a longer cooking time to soften them and release the pectin and acid. Simmer the fruits gently. Plums and blackcurrants should be cooked until their skins are soft. Once sugar is added, the skins may become tough if they haven't been cooked enough before.

Adding the sugar Use white granulated sugar. The amount of sugar needed varies, but the minimum amount recommended is 320 g/1⅜ cups sugar to 450 g/1 lb. of bulky fruit (or about 3½ cups of soft/bush fruits). Ideally, use 340–385 g (1½–1¾ cups) sugar for a soft-set jam and 450 g/2 cups sugar for a more traditional jam.

Warm the sugar in a bowl in the oven (for about 20 minutes on its lowest setting) before adding it to the fruit, as this will help it to dissolve quicker. Take the jam off the heat and allow it to cool slightly so it isn't still boiling when the sugar is added. Once the sugar has been added, stir continuously over low heat until the sugar has completely dissolved. (If the jam comes to the boil before the sugar has completely dissolved, it may crystallize during storage.)

Boiling the jam When the sugar has dissolved, turn up the heat and bring the jam to the boil. How long it needs to boil will vary, and this is something that becomes more apparent with experience. The jam needs to maintain a high temperature to reduce and thicken so it will set as it cools. Sometimes this can take a matter of minutes and on other occasions up to half an hour, depending on how much water the jam contains. This stage is often referred to as a rolling boil.

Testing for setting point After 5–10 minutes of rapid boiling, test the jam to see if it has reached setting point (see below). Remove the pan from the heat while testing, so the jam doesn't overcook.

The cold plate test Put a small plate in the freezer to chill beforehand. Drip a pool of jam onto the plate with a spoon and allow it to cool for a few seconds, then draw your finger through the jam. If setting point has been reached, the surface will wrinkle. When you raise your finger from the plate, the jam will form a strand, rather than dripping off.

Using a jam thermometer Dip the thermometer into hot water, then push it into the jam, preferably in the center of the pan. If the temperature reaches 105°C/220°F, setting point has been reached.

The flake test Dip a wooden spoon into the jam, then hold it above the pan. Leave it to cool for a few seconds, then let the jam fall off the spoon back into the pan. If the jam has a sticky consistency and forms strands or flakes that hang onto the spoon, setting point has been reached. If setting point has not been reached, place the pan back on the heat and continue to boil rapidly, testing again at 5-minute intervals.

Skimming During boiling, a scum sometimes forms on jam, jelly or marmalade due to bubbles rising to the surface. This scum is harmless but can spoil the look of the preserve. Stir in a small knob of butter to help disperse the scum or use a metal spoon to scoop it away.

Dispersing the fruit Whole fruits or large pieces of fruit often rise up to the top of a jam, and as the jam sets, they are likely to stay there. If you are making a softer-set jam with pieces in it, you may have to live with this, but for a thicker set, leave the jam for 5–10 minutes prior to placing in jars, then stir it to distribute the pieces more evenly.

Filling and storing Have your hot jars and jar funnel ready. Pour the jam into the jars, leaving 6mm/¼ inch between the top of the jam and the rim if you are using a mason jar; 12 mm/½ inch if you are sealing with paraffin wax and ordinary lids; or to the top if using waxed discs (see page 9). If using mason jars or other canning jars, follow the manufacturer's instructions for covering and sealing. Paraffin, if used, should be applied right away. Similarly, if using waxed discs, cover the jam with a waxed disc, push it down onto the surface, then screw on the lid, and leave the jar to cool. Jars which have been filled to the brim can be left to cool upside down, as this helps to produce a vacuum as the jam cools. Store the jam, once it is cool, in a dry, cool place.

Jam: the macerating method

Allowing fruit and sugar to macerate together before cooking draws the moisture and juices from the fruit and preserves the flavour. Cooking times are reduced and flavour is intensified, and it is possible to use a lower sugar content (see Adding the sugar, page 9), depending on the sweetness of the fruit.

Prepare the fruit as directed and place in a ceramic, glass, or stainless steel bowl. Add the sugar, cover with a plate, or push a piece of greaseproof/waxed paper down onto the surface of the fruit to hold in the moisture and leave to macerate: softer fruits for 6–8 hours and harder fruits for up to 36 hours. You will see the sugar soak up the juices and a considerable amount of liquid begin to dissolve the sugar.

Pour the fruit into a preserving pan and stir over a gentle heat until the sugar has completely dissolved. Occasionally, the mixture is left to macerate again; but if not, bring the jam to setting point as for the traditional method and pour into the jars.

Marmalade

If making citrus marmalade, it is important to cook the citrus rind properly, and this can take 1½–3 hours, depending on the method you choose. Ideally, poach the oranges whole, but you can remove the rind and shred it at the outset as an alternative. If you use waxed fruits, you will need to scrub them before use, but just a rinse will do for unwaxed ones.

Poaching Wash the whole fruits and place them in a heavy, lidded casserole with a tight-fitting lid. Pour in enough water to just cover the fruits, so they begin to float, then cover and place in an oven preheated to 180°C (350°F) Gas 4, to poach for 2½–3 hours, by which time the skins will be softened. Leave until cool enough to handle, then, using a slotted spoon, lift the fruits out, halve them, and scoop out the insides, gathering together all the pith and seeds and collecting any juice. Slice the rind into strips. Place the seeds and pith in a square of fine muslin/cheesecloth, and tie into a bundle with string. Pour any collected juice back in with the cooking liquid.

Paring the rind first Cut the uncooked fruits in half and squeeze out and collect the juice. Save the seeds. Pare the rind and chop into thin shreds. Chop the pith finely. Place the seeds in a square of muslin/cheesecloth and tie into a bundle with string. Place everything in a pan and add enough water to cover, then leave overnight to soak. The next day, bring to the boil, then simmer for about 1½ hours until the rind is softened and cooked through. Remove the bundle of seeds.

From now on, the method is the same whichever form of preparation you used. Add warmed sugar and stir to dissolve, then complete in the same way as if making jam. Once setting point is reached, leave the marmalade for 10–15 minutes, then remove the muslin/cheesecloth bag (if using the poaching method) and stir to distribute the rind shreds before pouring into jars.

Jellies

A jelly is similar to a jam but contains no fruit pieces. The fruit is cooked with water, then poured into a jelly bag and allowed to drip through. Only the juice is used. Fruits most suited are generally high in pectin (see page 6).

When making jellies, cook the fruit first with water until tender. You can mash the fruit with a spoon at this stage before pouring it into a jelly bag suspended over a container to catch the drips. For the clearest jelly, allow plenty of time for the juice to drip through (overnight is ideal), and don't squeeze the bag, as this makes the jelly cloudy. (It is often possible to reboil the contents of the jelly bag using half the original amount of water and pour it through the bag again to get the maximum amount of juice and pectin from the fruit.)

Now measure the juice to work out how much sugar will be needed. The general rule is 180 g/¾ cup sugar to every 240 ml/1 cup juice. The yield varies depending on the ripeness of the fruit and time allowed for dripping (thus how much juice is extracted). However, as a rough guide, 240 ml/1 cup juice should make 290 g/1¼ cups jelly. Place the juice in a preserving pan and add warmed sugar as for jam-making, stirring until completely dissolved. Bring to a rapid boil and cook on a high heat to reach settting point, as before.

Curds

These are made using sugar, butter and eggs and so are more like a custard than a jam, and are best suited to tart, fruity flavours. So that the eggs don't curdle or cook on too high a heat, use a double boiler or a basin set over a pan of simmering water. You must stir the curd continuously for 20–30 minutes until it thickens and will coat the back of the spoon; the effort will be well worth it.

First, make a purée by cooking the fruit in the minimum amount of water, if any, until tender. Softer fruits, such as raspberries and blueberries, require almost no cooking, but gooseberries and squash need more. Push the fruit through the fine disc of a food mill or a sieve to collect the purée.

Make curds in small jars: once opened, keep in the refrigerator and eat within 2 weeks. You can pour curds into suitable airtight containers and freeze them for up to 6 months.

Chutneys and pickles

Chutneys are made from fruits and vegetables mixed with vinegar, sugar and spices. They are easy to make, generally just requiring the ingredients to be put together in a preserving pan and cooked for a couple of hours. Pack chutneys and pickles in jars with vinegar-proof lids, and try to leave to mature for 6–8 weeks, or even a few months, before eating, as flavours mellow over time.

Most pickles and chutneys require vinegars flavoured with spices. However, you could also make your own pickling vinegar using the following recipe.

Pickling vinegar To 1 litre/1 quart cider, malt vinegar or wine vinegar, add the following: a piece of fresh ginger about 2 x 6.5 cm/¾ x 2½ in., peeled and finely sliced; 1 tablespoon each black peppercorns, mustard seeds and celery seeds; 8 dried red chillies; 2 teaspoons each whole allspice, whole cloves and whole coriander seeds.

Mix all the spices together and divide between clean, sterilized bottles. Fill the bottles with the vinegar and seal with corks or stoppers. Leave the vinegar to infuse for 6–8 weeks, giving the bottles an occasional shake. Strain out the spices before using.

Alternative method Place all the ingredients in a bowl and place this over a pan of simmering water, or use a double boiler. Allow the vinegar to warm through without boiling, then remove it from the heat and leave the spices to steep in the warm vinegar for 2–3 hours. Strain out the spices before using.

Keeping times

Jams and jellies will keep, unopened, in a cool, dark place for at least 6 months, but fruit curds have much shorter keeping times than jams and jellies – 2 months unopened in a cool place. The other preserves will keep unopened for 6–12 months. Keeping times once opened vary (for example, curds keep for 2 weeks once opened – see left).

Problem solving

Why jam goes mouldy Most often, the jam was not sealed adequately while still very hot. Or, jars were damp or cold when used, weren't filled to the top, or have been stored in a damp place. Mould is not harmful to the jam but it may affect the taste slightly. If it is removed, the jam can be boiled up again and re-packed in clean, sterilized jars.

Why tiny bubbles appear Bubbles indicate fermentation, usually due to too little sugar in relation to fruit quantity.

Why fruit rises in the jam When the fruit is in big pieces or is used whole, the pieces tend to rise in the jam after it is poured. To keep them dispersed throughout the preserve, leave the jam in the pan for 10–15 minutes after setting point is reached to thicken slightly, then stir before pouring it into the jars. The syrupy consistency of softer-set jams means that fruit will invariably rise. The same problem may occur with rind in marmalade, and the solution of waiting and stirring is the same in this case.

Why jam crystallizes Too much sugar or too little acid is usually the cause. Low-acid fruits benefit from the addition of acid in the form of lemon juice. Making sure that the sugar has dissolved completely before bringing the jam to a fast boil also helps. Sometimes overripe fruit is responsible, or storing the jam in too warm a place.

Why jam won't set Low levels of pectin, due to using fruits containing very little pectin or overripe fruit, may make it difficult to reach setting point. Other reasons include under-boiling the fruit, so that the pectin is not fully extracted, or insufficient evaporation of the water before the sugar is added, in which case return the jam to the preserving pan and boil it further. It is also possible to overcook jam after sugar has been added, for which there is no remedy.

Why jam shrinks in the jar Shrinkage is caused by the jam being inadequately covered or sealed, or failure to store it in a cool, dark, and dry place.

The term 'jam' describes fruit and sugar cooked together so it will keep, while jellies are clear, made with juice only, no fruit pieces. These easy recipes are so good you'll be tempted to eat them right off the spoon!

jams & jellies

strawberry & vanilla jam

Strawberry jam is the real classic. This fragile fruit isn't a great keeper, so for the best jam, capture the fruit at its freshest, preserving it in recognizable chunks. Here, strawberries are teamed with vanilla, their perfect partner. This recipe uses slightly less sugar than a traditional strawberry jam might and consequently has a softer set. Swirl a few spoonfuls through a mixture of mascarpone and plain yogurt for a fast dessert. Or dollop it onto a freshly baked scone.

1 vanilla bean

1 kg/2 lb. 4 oz. strawberries, hulled; larger fruits halved

750 g/3¾ cups sugar

freshly squeezed juice of 3 lemons

Makes 1.3 kg/3 lb.

Split the vanilla bean lengthways into four pieces and place in a bowl with the strawberries, tucking the pod pieces in among the fruit. Cover with the sugar and leave for 12 hours or overnight.

Pour the fruit, vanilla bean and juice into a preserving pan and add the lemon juice. Cook over a low heat until the sugar has dissolved, stirring only now and then so that the fruit stays intact. Turn up the heat and boil rapidly to reach setting point (see page 10). Skim if necessary (see page 10).

Remove the vanilla bean pieces, scrape the seeds out of them and add these to the jam, disposing of the pods. Stir the seeds through the jam.

Pour the jam into hot, sterilized jars (see page 8) and seal (see page 10).

tutti frutti jam

Mixed-fruit jams are a good way of using up small amounts of fruits that aren't in a great enough quantity to make jam on their own. You can also combine fruits with lower pectin levels with others that have a higher pectin content, which is an ideal way of helping the jam to set.

250 g/9 oz. blackcurrants

250 g/9 oz. redcurrants

250 g/9 oz. strawberries

250 g/9 oz. raspberries

1 kg/5 cups warmed sugar
(see page 10)

Makes 1.65 kg/3 lb. 10 oz.

Strip the black and redcurrants from their stalks by running the tines of a fork through the stems. Place the currants in a preserving pan with enough water just to stop the fruits catching on the bottom of the pan. Bring to the boil, then simmer for 15–20 minutes.

Add the strawberries and raspberries and simmer for a further 10 minutes. Add the warmed sugar to the fruit and stir over a low heat until all the sugar has dissolved. Turn up the heat and boil rapidly to reach setting point (see page 10). Skim if necessary (see page 10).

Pour the jam into hot, sterilized jars (see page 8) and seal (see page 10).

raspberry jam

Some people like jam with lots of seeds in it; some don't. With raspberry jam you have a choice. If you love the flavour of this fruit but find the seeds annoying, simply push the softened fruit through a sieve for a smoother finish. The result will taste just as good as the kind with the seeds in it.

1 kg/2 lb. 4 oz. raspberries

freshly squeezed juice of 1 lemon

800 g/4 cups warmed sugar
(see page 10)

Makes 1.3 kg/3 lb.

Place the raspberries and lemon juice in a preserving pan. Heat them gently to draw out the juice, mashing the berries with a spoon until the fruit is soft and there is plenty of juice. If you want a smooth jam, push the fruit through a sieve to remove the seeds.

Add the warmed sugar to the fruit and stir over a gentle heat until the sugar has completely dissolved. Turn up the heat and bring the jam to a fast boil until it reaches setting point (see page 10). Skim if necessary (see page 10).

Pour the jam into hot, sterilized jars (see page 8) and seal (see page 10).

plum jam

Most years, come late summer, plum trees are dripping with fruit; Blaisdon Red is a particularly good variety for this recipe, but many other varieties do well, too.

450 g/1 lb. plums, halved and stoned/pitted

450 g/2¼ cups warmed sugar (see page 10)

Makes 750 g/1 lb. 10 oz.

Place the plums in a pan with 100 ml/⅓ cup plus 1 tablespoon water and bring to a simmer, then cook gently for 10 minutes until the plums are soft but still intact.

Add the warmed sugar to the fruit and stir over a low heat until all the sugar has dissolved, then turn up the heat and boil rapidly to reach setting point (see page 10). Skim if necessary (see page 10).

Pour the jam into hot, sterilized jars (see page 8) and seal (see page 10).

700 g/1 lb. 9oz. raspberries

700 g/1 lb. 9oz. ripe peaches

1 kg/5 cups sugar

freshly squeezed juice of 2 large lemons

Makes 1.65 kg/3 lb. 10 oz.

peach & raspberry jam

This jam is wonderfully fragrant and gloriously colourful, with deep red raspberries dotted through with peach pieces.

Place the raspberries in a pan. Warm them gently to soften them and release their juice, mashing them with the back of a spoon. When they are soft and juicy, push them through the fine disc of a food mill or a sieve.

Place the raspberry purée, 500 g/1 lb. 2 oz. of the sugar and half of the lemon juice in a pan and bring to a simmer, then remove from the heat and pour into a ceramic or glass bowl. Cover the surface with greaseproof/waxed paper, pushed down onto the fruit, and leave the bowl in the refrigerator overnight.

Meanwhile, skin and stone/pit the peaches. Steep in boiling water for a few minutes, then drain and replace with cold water; they should now peel easily. Cut the flesh into quarters, then eighths, so the pieces are still quite chunky.

Place the peaches, and remaining sugar and lemon juice in a pan, bring just to simmering point, then remove from the heat. Pour the fruit into a glass or ceramic bowl; cover and refrigerate overnight as for the raspberries.

The next day, combine the raspberries and peaches in a preserving pan and heat gently, stirring all the time to be sure that the sugar has completely dissolved. Turn up the heat and boil rapidly until setting point is reached (see page 10). Skim if necessary (see page 10). Leave for 5 minutes, then stir to distribute the peach pieces. Pour the jam into hot, sterilized jars (see page 8) and seal (see page 10).

strawberry & gooseberry jam

Gooseberries and strawberries make a good partnership as the higher pectin levels found in gooseberries offset the lower levels in the strawberries. This unusual combination not only tastes great, but is colourful as well.

450 g/1 lb. gooseberries

450 g/1 lb. strawberries, hulled

900 g/4½ cups warmed sugar (see page 10)

freshly squeezed juice of 1 lemon

Makes 1.5 kg/3 lb. 5 oz.

Place the gooseberries in a preserving pan with 3 tablespoons of water. Heat gently and simmer until the berries are just soft, then add the strawberries. Cook for 5 minutes until the fruits begin to lose their shape and the juice starts to run.

Add the warmed sugar and the lemon juice to the fruit. Stir gently over a low heat until the sugar has completely dissolved. Turn up the heat and boil rapidly to reach setting point (see page 10). Skim if necessary (see page 10).

Pour the jam into hot, sterilized jars (see page 8) and seal (see page 10).

700 g/1 lb. 9 oz. cherries

500 g/2½ cups warmed sugar
(see page 10)

1 tablespoon freshly squeezed
lemon juice

Makes 900 g/2 lb.

cherry jam

You can use a black cooking cherry, such as a Morello cherry for this jam, or a paler dessert cherry and the colour of your jam will vary accordingly. If you grow your own, make sure to pick them as soon as they ripen or else the birds will eat the lot before you get the chance!

Stone/pit the cherries using a cherry stoner over a basin to catch any juice. Put the fruit and juice into a pan with 2 tablespoons water and simmer gently until the fruit is just cooked.

Add the warmed sugar and the lemon juice to the fruit and stir over a low heat until all the sugar has dissolved, then turn up the heat and boil rapidly to reach setting point (see page 10). Leave the jam for 5–10 minutes, then stir to redistribute the cherries. Skim if necessary (see page 10).

Pour the jam into hot, sterilized jars (see page 8) and seal (see page 10).

pear & vanilla jam

Once tasted, this jam is hard to live without. The specks of real vanilla dotted throughout the pale jam show its quality, infusing their aromatic flavour. Here, macerating the pears also brings out the most flavour from the fruit.

1 kg/2 lb. 4 oz. pears, peeled, cored and cut into chunky slices

freshly squeezed juice of 2 lemons

750 g/3¾ cups sugar

1 vanilla bean

Makes 1.3 kg/3 lbs.

Place the pears in a bowl with the lemon juice to stop them discolouring. Sprinkle the sugar over the fruit and add 200 ml/¾–1 cup water.

Slice the vanilla bean in half lengthways and scrape out the seeds, then tuck the pod in among the pears and add the seeds. Cover the bowl with a plate and leave overnight for the sugar to soak up some of the juices from the fruit.

The next day, pour the contents of the bowl into a preserving pan and stir over a low heat until the sugar has dissolved, then turn up the heat and boil rapidly to reach setting point (see page 10), by which time the pear pieces will be translucent. Skim if necessary (see page 10).

Remove the vanilla bean, then pour the jam into hot, sterilized jars (see page 8) and seal (see page 10).

green fig jam

Green or purple figs are suitable for jam making. Figs do not ripen any further once picked from the tree, and they don't have a massive flavour when unripe, so pick or buy them already ripe enough to use. This jam has a beautiful rich colour and is dotted throughout with seeds.

450 g/1 lb. figs, stalks removed and flesh chopped into small pieces

450 g/2¼ cups warmed sugar (see page 10)

freshly squeezed juice of 1 lemon

Makes 750 g/1 lb. 10 oz.

Place the figs in a pan with 2 tablespoons water, heat gently to a simmer and cook until soft and juicy.

Add the warmed sugar and the lemon juice to the fruit and stir over a low heat until all the sugar has dissolved, then turn up the heat and boil rapidly to reach setting point (see page 10). Leave for 10 minutes, then stir to distribute the fig pieces throughout the jam. Skim if necessary (see page 10).

Pour the jam into hot, sterilized jars (see page 8) and seal (see page 10).

white tea & apricot jam

Use apricots which are firm and unripe for this jam because the pectin levels are higher at this stage. White tea has a naturally peachy aroma, so it adds a lovely fragrant undertone here. Adding the apricot kernels is a good trick too and worth doing for the nutty perfume they exude.

750 g/1 lb. 10 oz. apricots

2 tablespoons silver tip white tea leaves or 3 silver tip white tea bags

200 ml/¾–1 cup just-boiled water

freshly squeezed juice of ½ a lemon

750 g/3¾ cups warmed sugar (see page 10)

Makes 1.25 kg/2 lb. 12 oz.

Halve the apricots and remove the stones/pits. Place them into a polythene freezer bag and whack with a rolling pin so the stones break and release the kernels. You only need 5–6 kernels so discard the rest.

Put the tea leaves (or bags) and hot water in a teapot and leave to steep for 3–4 minutes. Strain the white tea into a large preserving pan, add the apricots, kernels and lemon juice and bring to the boil. Cook the apricots for 20 minutes, or until they collapse. You can squash them with the back of your spoon to help break up any large pieces of fruit.

Pour the warmed sugar into the pan with the apricots and cook over low heat until the sugar has dissolved. Once the sugar has dissolved, turn up the heat and boil for about 15 minutes, or until setting point is reached (see page 10). Leave to cool for 20 minutes, then pour into hot, sterilized jars (see page 8) and seal while warm (see page 10).

green tomato jam

Usually thought of as an ingredient for chutney, green tomatoes were once popular for jam making but have somehow fallen from favour. This recipe proves that a fashion revival is due. The lemon peel and stem ginger work well here to produce a candied jam with an unusual colour.

finely pared rind and freshly squeezed juice of 1 lemon

500 g/1 lb. 2 oz. green tomatoes, finely chopped

400 g/2 cups sugar

2 pieces of stem ginger, finely sliced

Makes 700 g/1 lb. 9 oz.

Place the lemon rind in a pan with just enough water to cover it and simmer for about 1 hour until soft. Drain the rind, discarding the liquid.

Place the tomatoes and lemon juice in a bowl with the sugar and leave overnight for the sugar to soak up some of the juices from the fruit.

The next day, pour the contents of the bowl into a preserving pan and add the rind. Stir over a low heat until the sugar has dissolved, then turn up the heat and boil rapidly to reach setting point (see page 10). Skim if necessary (see page 10).

Stir in the stem ginger, then pour the jam into hot, sterilized jars (see page 8) and seal (see page 10).

peach & pear jam

This is another beautiful combination of delicate flavours. To cut down on the initial preparation and give a nice texture, use a food mill to process the fruits. If you prefer to leave the fruits in whole chunks, you will need to peel and core the pears and skin and stone/pit the peaches first.

500 g/1 lb. 2 oz. peaches, quartered and stoned/pitted

500 g/1 lb. 2 oz. pears, quartered

freshly squeezed juice of 1 lemon

850 g/4¼ cups sugar

Makes 1.3 kg/3 lb.

Place the fruit in a pan with the lemon juice plus 1 tablespoon water and heat gently to release the juices and soften the fruit. Simmer for 10 minutes, then remove from the heat and leave to cool.

Press the fruit mixture through the fine disc of a food mill or a sieve and collect the puréed pulp in a preserving pan. Add the sugar to the fruit and stir over a low heat until all the sugar has dissolved, then turn up the heat and boil rapidly to reach setting point (see page 10). Skim if necessary (see page 10).

Pour the jam into hot, sterilized jars (see page 8) and seal (see page 10).

apricot jam

This apricot jam contains a little less sugar than most, which gives it a softer set. Cooking time is kept to a minimum, preserving the flavour. Since the apricots are left in big chunks, these rise to the top – allocate one for each serving.

1 kg/2 lb. 4 oz. apricots
800 g/4 cups sugar
freshly squeezed juice of 1 lemon

Makes 1.3 kg/3 lb.

Skin the fruits by steeping them in boiling water for a few minutes, then replacing the hot water with cold. Keep the skins. Halve the fruits and remove the stones/pits. Place the skins and stones in a piece of muslin/cheesecloth and tie it into a bag.

Place the sugar and lemon juice in a ceramic or glass bowl and add 200 ml/¾–1 cup water; tuck the muslin/cheesecloth bag in among the other ingredients. Push a piece of greaseproof/waxed paper down onto the surface to cover it and refrigerate overnight to draw the juice out of the fruits.

The next day, pour the contents of the bowl into a preserving pan and heat gently, stirring until the sugar has completely dissolved. Simmer gently for 10 minutes without stirring so the apricot halves stay intact, then remove them from the syrup using a slotted spoon. Discard the muslin/cheesecloth bag.

Bring the syrup to the boil and boil rapidly to reach setting point (see page 10), then quickly put the apricots back into the syrup and bring to the boil again. Remove the jam from the heat. Skim if necessary (see page 10).

Spoon the apricots into hot, sterilized jars (see page 8), dividing them equally, then pour the syrup over them, filling the jars up to the top. Seal the jars (see page 11) and let cool upside down.

maple squash butter

1 kg/2 lb. 4 oz. butternut squash

100 ml/⅓ cup plus 1 tablespoon pure (unsweetened) apple juice

½–1 teaspoon ground ginger, to taste

7 tablespoons maple syrup

a cinnamon stick

Makes 600 ml/2½ cups

This is a slightly spicy, sweet golden spread for breakfast muffins, brioche, toast or warm bread rolls. If you like the warm, lemony flavour of preserved ginger, add 25 g/1 oz. stem ginger, drained and finely chopped, right at the end of the cooking time.

Preheat the oven to 180°C (350°F) Gas 4.

Halve the squash then scoop out the seeds. Set the two halves skin-side down in a baking dish. Cover tightly with foil then bake in the preheated oven until tender, about 1¼–1½ hours.

Remove the squash from the oven and leave until cool enough to handle. Peel off the skin and dice the flesh. Put the flesh into the bowl of a food processor with the apple juice, ground ginger, and maple syrup and process until smooth.

Tip the purée into a heavy pan, add the cinnamon stick, and set over medium heat. Bring to the boil, then cook until very thick, about 10 minutes, stirring very frequently to prevent the mixture from catching.

Spoon into hot sterilized jars (see page 8) and seal (see page 10).

apple butter

1.5 kg/3½ lb. mixed apples, such as Braeburn, Cox's and Bramley's, peeled, cored and chopped

350 g/12 oz. runny honey

200 g/1 cup sugar

2 tablespoons freshly squeezed lemon juice

1 teaspoon ground cinnamon

½ teaspoon ground cloves

250 ml/1 cup pure unsweetened apple juice

Makes about 1 kg/4 lb. 8 oz.

In America, apple jam is called Apple Butter. Use it as you would any fruit jam: on toast, with brioche, in sandwiches, drizzled over pancakes, or as a filling for sponge cakes.

Combine all the ingredients in a large non-reactive saucepan. Bring to the boil, stirring occasionally. Lower the heat and simmer, stirring occasionally and, using a wooden spoon, crush the apples, until thick, about 20–25 minutes. Remove from the heat.

Transfer the jam to a spotlessly clean and dry, sealable airtight container. It will keep in the refrigerator for 7–10 days. Alternatively, spoon into hot, dry sterilized jars while hot (see page 8). Let cool, then seal (see page 10). The jam will keep for 3–4 weeks if correctly sealed.

apple pumpkin jam

1 kg/2 lb. 4 oz. pumpkin, peeled, deseeded and diced

1 kg/2 lb. 4 oz. tart cooking apples, such as Bramley's, peeled, cored and chopped

freshly squeezed juice of ½ a lemon

500 g/2½ cups warmed sugar (see page 10)

1 teaspoon ground ginger

Makes about 1 litre/4 cups

This is an unusual and delicious conserve, and a handy recipe as it offers a use for retired Halloween jack o'lanterns.

Put all the ingredients in a preserving pan. Cook over medium heat, covered, for about 5–10 minutes to release the juices, then remove the lid and lower the heat.

Simmer for 40–50 minutes, stirring occasionally, and mashing the apples and pumpkin with a wooden spoon to break up the bigger pieces.

Let cool, then transfer the jam to a spotlessly clean and dry, sealable airtight container. It will keep in the refrigerator for up to 10 days. Alternatively, spoon into hot, dry sterilized jars while hot (see page 8). Let cool, then seal (see page 10). The jam will keep for 3–4 weeks if correctly sealed.

apple blackberry jam

600 g/1 lb. 5 oz. blackberries

625 g//1 lb. 6 oz. tart cooking apples, such as Bramley's, peeled, cored and chopped

450 g/2¼ cups warmed sugar (see page 10)

1 tablespoon freshly squeezed lemon juice

Makes about 1 litre/4 cups

This fruity jam is unbelievably simple to make but extraordinarily delicious.

Combine the blackberries, apples, sugar and lemon juice in a preserving pan. Stir over medium heat, until the sugar dissolves.

Continue cooking, stirring occasionally, until the fruit softens, about 20–30 minutes. Use a wooden spoon to crush the fruit slightly as you stir. Remove from the heat. Transfer the jam to a spotlessly clean and dry, sealable airtight container. It will keep in the refrigerator for 7–10 days. Alternatively, spoon into hot, dry sterilized jars while hot (see page 8). Let cool, then seal (see page 10). The jam will keep for 3–4 weeks if correctly sealed.

pineapple and apple jam

1 kg/2 lb. 4 oz. pineapple flesh

2 large cooking apples, peeled and cored

freshly squeezed juice of 1½ lemons

1 kg/5 cups sugar

8 green cardamom pods (optional)

Makes about 1 kg/2 lb. 4 oz.

This jam is very refreshing and the prettiest shade of lemon yellow. Try perking up some vanilla ice cream with a few spoonfuls of jam and a splash of rum. You could even paint a little rum on the inside of the wax seal before sealing the jars, just to give the jam a deliciously tropical taste.

Cut the pineapple and apples into tiny chunks. Weigh the fruit and transfer it to a large saucepan and sprinkle with lemon juice. Weigh or measure 85 g/⅓ cup sugar for every 100 g/3½ oz. of fruit and set aside. Add 150 ml/⅔ cup water to the fruit and simmer over low heat until the apple softens, 20–30 minutes. Meanwhile, split open the cardamom pods if using, and crush the seeds with a mortar and pestle. Add to the fruit as it cooks.

Add the weighed sugar to the pan and continue to cook over low heat until the sugar has dissolved, stirring all the while. Increase the heat and boil rapidly until setting point is reached (see page 10), 5–10 minutes. If the jam is not ready, put the pan back on the heat to boil for a few minutes longer and test again. Take the jam off the heat while testing; over-boiling will ruin it.

When setting point has been reached, skim the jam (see page 10), stir it well and let stand for 20 minutes for the fruit to settle. Stir and spoon into warm sterilized jars (see page 8) and seal (see page 10).

red fruit conserve

1 kg/2 lb. 4 oz. frozen
unsweetened red fruits

200 g/1 cup sugar

1 tablespoon freshly squeezed
lemon juice

340-g/12-oz. jar prepared
redcurrant jelly

Makes about 1 litre/4 cups

Frozen red fruits are available all year round and always make a useful addition to the freezer. This recipe, made with raspberries, strawberries, cherries, blueberries, redcurrants and blackcurrants, makes a juicy, thick conserve to serve warm or at room temperature with pancakes and waffles, ice cream, muffins or brioche.

Put the frozen fruits, sugar, lemon juice and redcurrant jelly into a large non-metallic bowl. Cover and leave for 2–4 hours, or overnight in the refrigerator, until the fruit has thawed.

Tip the mixture into a preserving pan and bring to the boil. Simmer steadily until the mixture has thickened, about 10 minutes. Remove the pan from the heat, stir gently, then spoon the jam into sterilized jars (see page 8) and seal (see page 10).

dried apricot conserve

500 g/1 lb. 2 oz. dried apricots
(soaked weight 1 kg/2 lb. 4 oz.)

freshly squeezed juice of 1 lemon

1 kg/5 cups warmed sugar
(see page 10)

50 g/½ cup walnut halves, each
broken into 4 pieces

2 tablespoons Amaretto di
Saronno or other almond-flavoured
liqueur (optional)

Makes about 1 kg/2 lb. 4 oz.

Apricots make one of the most luxurious preserves of all.
The apricot season is fairly short, but this useful recipe
uses dried apricots. They need soaking well, then long, slow
cooking to soften them. You could also use fresh apricots.

Cut the apricots in half, put in a large bowl, cover with cold
water, add the lemon juice and set aside for 24 hours.

Strain off the juice into a measuring jug and make up to
1 litre/4 cups with cold water. Put the fruit in a heavy pan, add
the juice and water and simmer over low heat for 30 minutes
or until quite soft. The fruit can be mashed at this stage or left
in pieces.

Add the sugar and bring slowly to simmering point. Cook gently,
stirring until dissolved. Increase the heat and boil hard for 10
minutes, add the walnut pieces and return to a fast boil.

Take the pan off the heat and test for set (see page 10). When
setting point has been reached, add the Amaretto if using, return
to the boil, stir and skim (see page 10) if necessary. Let the jam
rest for 20 minutes, then stir well and ladle into hot sterilized
jars (see page 8) and seal (see page 10).

italian fig conserve

Make sure you use only plump, firm fruit for this delicious preserve. You can use green figs, but they should be peeled first. It is perfect with crusty bread and butter, brioche, or toast for breakfast, but would also make excellent jam tartlets or Italian crostata.

1.5 kg/3 lb. firm black figs

freshly squeezed juice of 2 lemons

1.2 kg/6 cups warmed sugar (see page 10)

7-g/¼-oz. envelope vanilla sugar (optional)

Makes about 1 kg/2 lb. 4 oz.

Wipe the figs and chop into tiny pieces. Put in a saucepan with the lemon juice and 200 ml/¾ cup water. Cook over low heat until soft – this may take 20–30 minutes, but if the skins are not cooked until tender at this stage, they will be tough when boiled with the sugar. Add the sugar and cook over low heat until dissolved. Stir in the vanilla sugar, increase the heat and boil until setting point is reached (see page 10), 5–10 minutes.

Take the pan off the heat and test for set. If the jam is not ready, put the pan back on the heat to boil for a few minutes longer and test again. Repeat this process if necessary and remember to take the jam off the heat while testing, because over-boiling will ruin it.

When setting point has been reached, skim the jam (see page 10), stir it well and let stand for 20 minutes for the fruit to settle. Stir and ladle into warm sterilized jars (see page 8). Seal at once (see page 10). Let cool, label and store in a cool, dark cupboard.

peppermint tea & apple jelly

This is a great jelly for serving with roast lamb. You could also add some fresh chopped mint once the whole thing is cooked before transferring into jars.

6 peppermint tea bags

1 kg/4 lb. 8 oz. cooking apples, unpeeled, washed and roughly chopped

100 ml/⅓ cup plus 1 tablespoon cider vinegar

1 kg/5 cups warmed sugar (see page 10)

a jelly bag or muslin/cheesecloth

Makes 1.5 kg/3 lb. 5 oz.

Put 1 litre/4 cups water in a preserving pan and bring to the boil. Add the tea bags, remove from the heat and leave to steep for 5 minutes. Discard the tea bags.

Add the apples (cores and peel included) to the pan and cover. Cook gently over low heat for about 1 hour, until very tender and collapsed. Add the vinegar and remove from the heat.

Transfer the apple pulp to a jelly bag suspended over a bowl and leave it alone for about 30 minutes, or until it stops dripping. Discard the pulp in the jelly bag. (You can use a large piece of muslin/cheesecloth gathered into a bag and tied with string).

Measure the juice you have collected (you should have about 1.4 litres/6 cups) and add the warmed sugar. If your yield of juice is different, adjust the amount of sugar to the ratio of 70 g/⅓ cup sugar to 100 ml/⅓ cup clear juice. Return the mixture to a pan set over low heat and let the sugar dissolve slowly. Stir occasionally. Once the sugar has dissolved, turn up the heat and boil for about 15 minutes, or until setting point is reached (see page 10). Leave to cool for 20 minutes, then pour into warm sterilized jars (see page 8) and seal (see page 10).

blackcurrant jelly

1 kg/2 lb. 4 oz. blackcurrants, stripped from their stalks

freshly squeezed juice of 1 lemon (optional)

warmed sugar (see page 10; for quantity see method)

a jelly bag or muslin/cheesecloth

Makes 750 g/1 lb. 10 oz.

Blackcurrants have an unmistakable and robust taste that makes them ideal for jams and jellies. This jelly is deep black and glassy, with a perfectly balanced rich, yet tart, flavour. (If you prefer a slightly less tart version you can omit the lemon juice.) This one is especially suitable for anyone who prefers a smooth, 'no bits' spread.

Place the currants in a preserving pan with the lemon juice, if using, and 600 ml/2½ cups water and simmer for 5 minutes, until the currants start to burst and the juice flows. Remove from the heat and squash the currants with the tines of a fork.

Pour the currants and liquid into a jelly bag suspended over a bowl and leave it to drip for several hours or overnight. (You can use a large piece of muslin/cheesecloth gathered into a bag and tied with string).

As blackcurrants have a high pectin content (see page 6), you can increase the yield by tipping the pulp back into the pan, along with 300 ml/1¼ cups water, and boiling it for 5 minutes. Pour the pulp back into the jelly bag and leave it to drain for a few hours to extract the juice, collecting it in a measuring jug.

Heat the juice in a preserving pan set over low heat, then add the warmed sugar (allow 450 g/2¼ cups sugar for every 600 ml/2½ cups juice). Stir until the sugar has completely dissolved, then turn up the heat and boil rapidly until setting point is reached (see page 10). Skim if necessary (see page 10). Pour into hot, sterilized jars (see page 8) and seal (see page 10).

easy chilli jam

This recipe couldn't be easier. Whizz everything in a blender, then let it bubble up to a thick, glossy, irresistible conserve that is great with grills, cold meats and cheeses, and is a boon in the kitchen when it comes to adding a little pizzazz to sauces, stir-fries and the like.

1 kg/2 lb. 4 oz. ripe tomatoes, quartered

6 red fresh chillies/chiles
(or less or more to taste)

3-cm/1¼-inch piece of fresh ginger, peeled and finely grated

100 ml/⅓ cup plus 1 tablespoon white wine vinegar

250 g/1¼ cups sugar

2 tablespoons extra virgin olive oil

Makes 750 g/1 lb. 10 oz.

Put the tomatoes and chillies/chiles in a food processor and blend to a purée. Pour into a preserving pan with the ginger, vinegar and sugar, and stir over medium heat until the sugar has dissolved. Leave to bubble for a further 30 minutes, or until reduced and thickened.

Add the olive oil and cook for 10–15 minutes, or until the mixture has the consistency of jam. Remove from the heat, leave to cool, then spoon into sterilized jars (see page 8) and refrigerate until needed.

1 kg/2 lb. 4 oz. white currants, stripped from their stalks

4 red gooseberries (optional)

freshly squeezed juice of 1 lemon

2 fresh red chillies/chiles (or more or less to taste), deseeded and finely chopped

warmed sugar (see page 10; for quantity see method)

Makes 1.3 kg/3 lb.

white currant & red chilli jam

White currants are another fruit with a lovely tart flavour, which makes them just perfect for jam making. This jam, with its additional chilli kick, is subtle enough to eat on sourdough toast for breakfast but could also be taken up a notch, by adding more chilli to taste, and serving as a relish to go with cheese. And if you have a few red gooseberries to add to the currants, they'll give this jam a beautiful rose hue.

Place the currants and gooseberries, if using, in a preserving pan along with the lemon juice and 150 ml/⅔ cup water. Simmer until the fruits are soft and bursting.

Push the fruit through the fine disc of a food mill or a sieve, collecting the resulting purée in a measuring jug.

Allow 450 g/2¼ cups sugar to every 600 ml/2½ cups purée.

Gently heat the purée and add the chopped chillies/chiles, then add the warmed sugar. Stir the jam over a low heat until the sugar has completely dissolved. Turn up the heat and boil rapidly to reach setting point (see page 10). Skim if necessary (see page 10).

Pour the jam into hot, sterilized jars (see page 8) and seal (see page 10).

Many people consider a breakfast incomplete without toast and marmalade.
Fruit curds contain eggs and are best suited to tart flavours, making them
another popular choice for the morning, but they also work well in desserts.

marmalades & curds

seville orange marmalade

Because of their bitter taste Seville oranges are used only for cooking, but this robust quality is what makes them particularly good for making marmalade.

1 kg/2 lb. 4 oz. Seville oranges

1 unwaxed lemon

1.5 kg/7½ cups sugar

a jelly bag or muslin/cheesecloth

Makes 2 kg/4 lb. 8 oz.

Preheat the oven to 180°C (350°F) Gas 4. Place the whole fruits in a heavy, lidded casserole that will fit in the oven, cover with water and poach as described on page 11.

Lift the fruit out of the liquid into a colander. When cool enough to handle, cut each fruit in half and scoop out the pulp with a spoon, leaving just the peel, placing the pulp, pith and pips, in a jelly bag suspended over a bowl to catch any drips. (You can use a large piece of muslin/cheesecloth gathered into a bag and tied with string). Measure the liquid, adding any collected in the bowl under the drained pulp, and if necessary add water to make it up to 1 litre/4 cups.

Place the bag in a saucepan with enough poaching liquid to cover. Bring to the boil and simmer for 15 minutes. Leave until cool enough to handle, then squeeze the bag to get as much liquid as possible from the pulp. Discard the bag and contents.

Chop the rind into thin strips and put into a preserving pan. Add all the poaching liquid. If the mixture is cold, you can add the sugar without warming it; otherwise you will need to warm the sugar first (see page 10). Stir the sugar into the orange liquid over a low heat until completely dissolved and the liquid is clear, then boil rapidly for 15 minutes and test for setting point (see page 10). Turn off the heat and leave the marmalade to stand for 15 minutes, then stir to distribute the peel. Skim if necessary (see page 10). Pour into hot, sterilized jars (see page 8) and seal (see page 10).

orange & kumquat marmalade

Cut the orange rind into very thin strips with a sharp citrus zester. Put the rind in a large bowl. Cut away the pith and put in a second large bowl. Cut the orange into segments and reserve the segment skin, pips and central core of the orange, taking care to save any juice. Add the segments and orange and lemon juices to the bowl of rind. Add the reserved skin, pips and core of the orange to the bowl of pith.

Cut the kumquats in half lengthways, scrape out all the flesh, pith and pips with a teaspoon. Add this to the orange pith. Cut the rind into thin strips and add to the bowl with the orange rind. Add 500 ml/2 cups water to the bowl of fruit and add another 500 ml/2 cups water to the pith and pips. Cover both bowls with a clean cloth and let steep overnight or for 24 hours.

Put the pith and pips in a pan and simmer, covered, over low heat for 30 minutes. Transfer to a jelly bag set over a bowl and let drain for 30 minutes. (You can use a large piece of muslin/cheesecloth gathered into a bag and tied with string). Squeeze the bag to extract the remaining liquid.

Pour the fruit, zest and water into a preserving pan, then add the extracted liquid from the pith. Put over low heat, bring slowly to simmering point and cook until the zest softens and the liquid has reduced by half. Warm the sugar (see page 10) and add to the pan. Stir the sugar into the liquid over a low heat until completely dissolved and the liquid is translucent, then increase the heat, bring to the boil and boil rapidly for 5–10 minutes and test for setting point (see page 10). Take the pan off the heat and test for set (see page 10). When setting point has been reached, add the honey, return to simmering point, then turn off the heat. Skim if necessary (see page 10). Pour into hot, sterilized jars (see page 8) and seal (see page 10).

3 sweet oranges, scrubbed

115 g/4 oz. kumquats, scrubbed

600 g/3 cups sugar

freshly squeezed juice of ½ a lemon

1 tablespoon honey

a jelly bag or muslin/cheesecloth

Makes about 750 g/1 lb. 10 oz.

quince & orange marmalade

Reputedly, the original marmalade was a preserve made from quinces, and the name comes from the word *marmelo*, the Portuguese word for this Mediterranean fruit.

1 kg/2 lb. 4 oz. quinces, fur washed off

3 unwaxed oranges

warmed sugar (see page 10; for quantity see method)

Makes about 1.5 kg/3 lb. 5 oz.

Place the fruits in a lidded casserole dish and pour in enough boiling water to cover the fruits so they just begin to float. Put on the lid and slow cook in the oven for 6–8 hours or overnight.

Remove from the oven and leave until cool enough to handle. Strain the liquid through a colander into a preserving pan. Peel the quinces, quarter them and remove the cores, then place the skins and cores in with the cooking liquid. Cut 2 of the oranges in half, scoop out the flesh and add the pips and pith to the liquid as well. Put the peel to one side.

Bring the mixture to the boil and reduce it down to about a third or a half of the original quantity. Pour the reduced mixture through a sieve into a preserving pan.

Cut the quinces into chunky slices about 2-cm/¾-inch square and 1-cm/½-inch thick. Slice the whole orange into thin rounds and chop the empty orange halves into fine shreds.

Weigh the quince, orange slices and shredded rind, add them to the reduced mixture and warm through. Add the same weight of warmed sugar and stir over a low heat until all the sugar has dissolved, taking care to keep the orange slices intact, then turn up the heat and boil rapidly to reach setting point (see page 10). Skim if necessary (see page 10). Remove the orange slices with a slotted spoon and use them to decorate the insides of hot, sterilized jars (see page 8) by standing them on end against the glass. Pour the marmalade into the jars and seal (see page 10).

chunky lemon, lime & grapefruit marmalade

1 unwaxed lemon

1 small unwaxed pink grapefruit

1 unwaxed lime

500 ml/2 cups water

1 kg/5 cups sugar

freshly squeezed juice of ½ a lemon

Makes about 750 g/1 lb. 10 oz.

The beauty of this marmalade is that it can be made in small quantities at any time of the year, not just when Seville oranges are in season.

Scrub the fruit and prise out any stalk ends still attached. Put in a preserving pan and cover with cold water. Set over low heat and cook until tender – this will take 1½–2 hours. The fruit is ready when it 'collapses'. Lime rind is much tougher than other citrus peel, so you must make sure it is tender at this stage.

Transfer the fruit to a chopping board and leave until cool enough to handle. Cut in half, scrape out all the flesh and pips and add to the pan of water. Bring to the boil and simmer for 5 minutes. Cut the rind into strips as thin as possible. Strain the water from the pips and flesh and return it to the pan, adding the chopped rind and lemon juice. Discard the pips and debris.

Stir the sugar into the liquid over a low heat until completely dissolved and the liquid is translucent, then increase the heat, bring to the boil and boil rapidly for 5–10 minutes. Take the pan off the heat and test for set (see page 10). When setting point has been reached, add the honey, return to simmering point, then turn off the heat. Skim if necessary (see page 10). Pour into hot, sterilized jars (see page 8) and seal (see page 10).

apple & blackcurrant marmalade

500 g/1 lb. 2 oz. blackcurrants

500 g/1 lb. 2 oz. apples, cut into large chunks

warmed sugar (see page 10; for quantity see method)

Makes 1.3 kg/3 lb.

Although this marmalade doesn't contain any citrus fruits, the blackcurrants give just the right amount of tartness and punch to make it a perfect preserve for serving at breakfast.

Strip the blackcurrants from their stalks by running the tines of a fork through the stems.

Place all the fruit together in a pan with about 3 tablespoons water (just enough to keep the fruit from catching on the bottom of the pan). Simmer gently until the fruit is soft, the juices flow and the apples are fluffy. Remove from the heat and leave until cool enough to handle.

Press the fruit mixture through the fine disc of a food mill or a sieve into a bowl. Weigh the purée, then pour it into a preserving pan and add an equal weight of warmed sugar. Stir over a low heat until all the sugar has dissolved, then turn up the heat and boil rapidly to reach setting point (see page 10). Skim if necessary (see page 10).

Pour the marmalade into hot, sterilized jars (see page 8) and seal (see page 10).

lemon & fig marmalade

This unusual combination is well worth trying. The lemon half-moons are left in large chunks which give a lovely candied tang to the preserve. Along with the figs, they make a great start to the day.

450 g/1 lb. dried figs

3 unwaxed lemons

1.1 kg/5¼ cups warmed sugar (see page 10)

Makes 1.5 kg/3 lb. 5 oz.

Remove the stalks from the figs and cut each into 4 chunks. Halve the lemons lengthways, then slice the halves thinly, collecting all the juice and any pips. Place the pips in a piece of muslin/cheesecloth and tie it into a bag with string. Place the lemon slices and juice, the figs and the wrapped pips in a large bowl, cover them with 1.1 litres/5 cups water and leave for 24 hours.

Pour the mixture into a pan and heat to simmering; leave simmering for 1–1½ hours until the lemon rind is soft. Leave to cool slightly and remove the pips.

Add the warmed sugar. Stir over a low heat, without boiling, until the sugar has completely dissolved, then bring the marmalade to a rapid boil and cook until it reaches setting point (see page 10). Skim if necessary (see page 10).

Pour into hot, sterilized jars (see page 8) and seal (see page 10).

peach marmalade

900 g/2 lbs. peaches, roughly chopped

750 g/3¾ cup warmed sugar (see page 10)

Makes 1.3 kg/3 lb.

This aromatic, slightly gentler marmalade can be enjoyed just about any time of day. The cooking brings out the superb aroma of the fruit – add some vanilla for an even more sybaritic experience.

Place the peaches and their stones/pits in a pan along with 250 ml/1 cup water. Bring them to simmering point and simmer until the peach pieces are soft.

Discard the stones/pits and press the flesh through the fine disc of a food mill or a sieve, to give a purée.

Put the purée into a preserving pan, add the warmed sugar, and stir gently over a low heat until the sugar has completely dissolved. Turn up the heat and boil until it reaches setting point (see page 10). Skim if necessary (see page 10).

Pour the marmalade into hot, sterilized jars (see page 8) and seal (see page 10).

grapefruit & lime curd

This curd may taste a little sweet when first made, but it will lose sweetness once it is cold. Choose the best-quality organic eggs when making curds as they help to give a brighter colour to the finished product. Also, it is well worth taking the time to strain the beaten eggs as there is often a surprising amount of residue left in the strainer.

1 unwaxed grapefruit

2 unwaxed limes

4 eggs, well beaten

275 g/1½ cups minus 2 tablespoons caster/superfine sugar

Makes about 500 g/1 lb. 2 oz.

Wash and dry the fruit. Finely grate the rind of the grapefruit and 1 of the limes. Squeeze the juice, strain and measure 4 tablespoons lime juice and 125 ml/½ cup grapefruit juice.

Put the eggs in a bowl and whisk them lightly. Put the strained juices, grated rind and sugar in a bowl and place over a pan of simmering water (or use a double boiler).

Strain the beaten eggs into the mixture and stir over a very low heat until the sugar has dissolved and the mixture begins to thicken. Continue stirring until the mixture is thick enough to coat the back of a wooden spoon, about 20–40 minutes.

For a very smooth preserve, strain through a fine sieve into a measuring jug, then pour the curd into small, hot, sterilized jars (see page 8) and seal (see page 10).

apricot curd

Fresh home-grown apricots cannot be bettered, but even a punnet-full from the supermarket will make tasty curd. Curd makes an extra special gift if you also include a packet of small meringues or mini pastry cases.

225 g/8 oz. apricots, quartered and stoned/pitted

2 eggs, well beaten

rind and freshly squeezed juice of 1 unwaxed lemon

50 g/½ stick unsalted butter, cut into cubes

225 g/1 cup plus 2 tablespoons caster/superfine sugar

Makes 500 g/1 lb. 2 oz.

Place the apricots in a pan with about 2 tablespoons water (just enough to stop the fruit from catching on the bottom of the pan) and cook gently until soft.

Cool the fruit slightly, then press it through the fine disc of a food mill or a sieve, collecting the resulting purée in a bowl.

Strain the beaten eggs through a sieve into the purée. Add the lemon rind and juice, the butter and the sugar. Place the bowl over a pan of simmering water (or use a double boiler).

Cook gently, stirring continuously with a wooden spoon, until the mixture is completely blended and thickens enough to coat the back of the spoon. This should take about 30 minutes.

For a very smooth preserve, strain through a fine sieve into a measuring jug, then pour the curd into small, hot, sterilized jars (see page 8) and seal (see page 10).

lemon curd

2 large unwaxed lemons

125 g/1 stick unsalted butter, cut into cubes

175 g/¾ cup plus 2 tablespoons caster/superfine sugar

3 eggs, well beaten

Makes 500 g/1 lb. 2 oz.

This is a quintessentially British preserve, tart yet sweet and buttery at the same time. Delicious on toast or on freshly made scones or bread, it makes an excellent filling for tarts, sponge cakes or meringues.

Finely grate the lemon rind into a heatproof bowl. Squeeze the juice and add that to the bowl with the butter and sugar.

Place the bowl over a pan of simmering water (or use a double boiler). Cook gently, stiring with a wooden spoon until the butter melts. Add the egg and stir the mixture for 10–15 minutes until the mixture thickens noticeably and takes on a translucent look.

For a very smooth preserve, strain through a fine sieve into a measuring jug, then pour the curd into small, hot, sterilized jars (see page 8) and seal (see page 10).

raspberry curd

Raspberries give this delicious curd a wonderful colour and a lovely tangy taste. Save small, unusual-shaped glass jars especially for potting up curds, since they are great to give as pretty homemade gifts.

250 g/9 oz. raspberries

175 g/¾ cup plus 2 tablespoons caster/superfine sugar

50 g/½ stick unsalted butter, cut into cubes

2 eggs, well beaten

Makes 350 g/12 oz.

Place the raspberries in a pan and cook them gently for 5–10 minutes, squashing the fruits with a spoon to help release the juice.

Push the fruit through a sieve, collecting the purée in a bowl.

Place the bowl over a pan of simmering water (or use a double boiler) and add all the other ingredients, pouring the beaten eggs through a sieve onto the purée. Stir with a wooden spoon until everything is well blended. Continue cooking, stirring constantly, until the curd is thick enough to coat the back of the spoon – this should take about 20–30 minutes.

For a very smooth preserve, strain through a fine sieve into a measuring jug, then pour the curd into small, hot, sterilized jars (see page 8) and seal (see page 10).

bitter orange curd

The bitter nature of Seville oranges works perfectly for a curd. Most sweet oranges just don't have enough character to use in this way, although blood oranges have more of a flavour kick than other sweet varieties, so they work well also. Use the curd as a filling for a sweet pastry tart, or spread it liberally to sandwich the layers of a rich chocolate cake, or simply serve it on a thick slice of fresh bread.

zest and freshly squeezed juice of 3 unwaxed Seville oranges

50 g/½ stick unsalted butter, cut into cubes

175 g/¾ cup plus 2 tablespoons caster/superfine sugar

2 eggs, well beaten

Makes 350 g/12 oz.

Finely grate the orange zest into a heatproof bowl. Squeeze the juice and add that to the bowl with the butter and sugar.

Place the bowl over a pan of simmering water (or use a double boiler). Cook gently, stiring with a wooden spoon until the butter melts. Add the egg and stir the mixture for 10–15 minutes until the mixture thickens noticeably and takes on a translucent look.

For a very smooth preserve, strain through a fine sieve into a measuring jug, then pour the curd into small, hot, sterilized jars (see page 8) and seal (see page 10).

blueberry & lime curd

The best and tastiest blueberries err on the tart side and here these berries benefit from an added boost with the addition of the rind and freshly squeezed juice of a lime.

225 g/8 oz. blueberries

zest and freshly squeezed juice of 1 unwaxed lime

50 g/½ stick unsalted butter, cut into cubes

225 g/1 cup plus 2 tablespoons caster/superfine sugar

2 eggs, well beaten

Makes 450 g/1 lb.

Place the blueberries in a pan with the lime rind and juice and cook gently for 5–10 minutes until tender. Purée the fruit and push it through a sieve, collecting the purée in a bowl.

Place the bowl over a pan of simmering water (or use a double boiler) and add all the other ingredients, pouring the beaten eggs through a sieve onto the purée. Stir with a wooden spoon until everything is well blended. Continue cooking, stirring constantly, until the curd is thick enough to coat the back of the spoon – this should take about 20–30 minutes.

For a very smooth preserve, strain through a fine sieve into a measuring jug, then pour the curd into small, hot, sterilized jars (see page 8) and seal (see page 10).

Homemade chutneys are a great thing to keep on hand, and are so easy to make it is amazing that anyone ever buys them in a store. Serve with cheese, on sandwiches or baked potatoes, and with roast meats, both hot and cold.

chutneys & savoury preserves

apple, pear & ginger chutney

3 eating apples, such as Golden Delicious, peeled, cored and diced

2 large ripe pears, peeled, cored and diced

1 large white onion, finely chopped

375 ml/1½ cups plus 1 tablespoon cider vinegar

350 g/1¾ cups light brown sugar

100 g/¾ cup sultanas/golden raisins or raisins

140-g/5-oz. piece of fresh ginger, peeled and finely chopped

½ teaspoon salt

½ teaspoon dried red chilli/hot pepper flakes

Makes 1–1.4 litres/4–6 cups

This chutney is especially good served with roast pork.

In a preserving pan, combine all the ingredients and cook over medium heat, stirring occasionally, until the mixture is thick, about 30–40 minutes.

Transfer the chutney to a clean and dry, sealable airtight container. It will keep in the refrigerator for up to 2 weeks.

apple, red onion & dried cherry chutney

3 eating apples, such as Golden Delicious, peeled, cored and diced

1 large or 2 medium red onions, halved and sliced

175 g/1½ cups dried sour cherries

500 ml/2 cups cider vinegar

3 tablespoons light brown sugar

¼ teaspoon ground cloves

¼ teaspoon salt

freshly ground black pepper

Makes 500–750 ml/2–3 cups

This chutney goes very well with poultry: chicken, turkey and even duck.

In a preserving pan, combine all the ingredients and cook over medium heat, stirring occasionally, until the mixture is thick, about 30–40 minutes.

Transfer the chutney to a clean and dry, sealable airtight container. It will keep in the refrigerator for up to 2 weeks.

grannie's apple chutney

This chutney is renowned – and the best thing is, like most chutneys, it is very simple to make. Serve in pork sandwiches, with all kinds of eggs, cheese, cold meats or an English cooked breakfast.

1 kg/2 lb. 4 oz. cooking apples, peeled and cored

500 g/1 lb. 2oz. onions

125 g/1 cup raisins

125 g/1 cup sultanas/golden raisins

500 g/2½ cups demerara sugar

½ teaspoon cayenne pepper

½ teaspoon hot dry mustard

½ teaspoon ground ginger

1 tablespoon plus 2 teaspoons salt

500 ml/2 cups malt vinegar, plus 500 ml/2 cups extra to add as the chutney boils down

Makes 1.5–2.25 kg/3 lb. 5 oz.–5 lb.

Chop the apples and onions very finely – this can be done in a food processor, but take care not to reduce it a pulp. It is important for the chutney to have texture.

Put the apples, onions, raisins, sultanas/golden raisins, sugar, cayenne, mustard, ginger, salt and the 500 ml/2 cups malt vinegar in a preserving pan and simmer for 1–1½ hours over low to medium heat. Stir regularly to make sure the sugar does not burn, adding extra vinegar as necessary as the chutney reduces.

Turn off the heat and let the chutney settle. Stir and transfer to a warm sterilized jar (see page 8), cover the surface of the chutney with a waxed disc and seal at once (see page 10).

Keep at least 1 month before you try it. This kind of chutney improves with age. After opening, keep covered in the refrigerator and use within 2 months.

400 g/14 oz. peeled and deseeded firm pumpkin or butternut squash flesh, cut into 1-cm/½-inch cubes

200 g/7 oz. ripe tomatoes, skinned, deseeded and chopped

200 g/7 oz. white onions, chopped

25 g/¼ cup sultanas/golden raisins

250 g/1¼ cups demerara/brown sugar

1 teaspoon salt

3-cm/1¼-inch piece of fresh ginger, peeled and finely chopped

1 garlic clove, finely chopped

freshly grated nutmeg

200 ml/¾ cup malt vinegar, plus 100 ml/⅓ cup extra to add as the chutney boils down

Makes 500 g/1 lb. 2 oz.

pumpkin & red tomato chutney

There are many varieties of pumpkin and this recipe can be used to preserve all of them. Make sure that the flesh is firm and not stringy, or it will spoil the finished texture of the chutney. Serve with a ploughman's lunch, scrambled eggs or cold meats.

Put the pumpkin, tomatoes, onions, sultanas/golden raisins, sugar, salt, ginger, garlic, nutmeg and the 200 ml/¾ cup vinegar in a preserving pan and bring slowly to the boil. Simmer for 1 hour, stirring from time to time. The chutney should look dark, dense and rich. Top up with extra vinegar if the chutney dries out too much while cooking.

Transfer to a warm sterilized jar (see page 8), cover the surface of the chutney with a waxed disc, and seal at once (see page 10). Keep for 1–6 months before opening. After opening, keep covered in the refrigerator and use within 2 months.

900 g/2 lb. butternut squash or pumpkin

2 large aubergines/eggplants (about 500 g/1 lb. 2 oz.)

650 g/1 lb. 7 oz. onions, chopped

4 garlic cloves, crushed

2–3 fresh red chillies/chiles, deseeded and thinly sliced or finely chopped

1 tablespoon each crushed coriander seeds and brown mustard seeds

finely grated zest and freshly squeezed juice of 1 unwaxed orange

50-g/1¾-oz. piece of fresh ginger

400 ml/1¾ cups cider vinegar or white wine vinegar

400 g/2 cups sugar, warmed (see page 10)

2 teaspoons salt, plus extra to taste

cayenne or chilli powder, to taste

Makes about 1.5 kg/4 lb.

squash & aubergine chutney

This golden chutney is flecked with dark purple and the red of the chilli peppers. Use white sugar to preserve the colours of the squash or pumpkin, and brown sugar for a deeper colour and flavour. Serve it with bread and cheese, ham and cured meats or spread on a sandwich.

Cut the squash and aubergines/eggplant into 1–2-cm/½–1-inch dice and place in a preserving pan with the onions, garlic, chillies/chiles, crushed coriander and mustard seeds and the orange zest and juice. Bash the ginger with a rolling pin to bruise it, tie it in a piece of muslin/cheesecloth and bury it in the mixture. Pour over the vinegar. Bring to the boil, then simmer very gently, part-covered, for 40–50 minutes until the squash is fully tender. Stir in the warmed sugar and the 2 teaspoons salt, stir until the sugar dissolves, then bring to the boil and cook briskly, stirring every few minutes, until the mixture is thick and the liquid almost all absorbed, about 30–40 minutes. Stir very frequently towards the end of cooking to stop the mixture sticking to the base of the pan.

It is ready when a wooden spoon drawn over the base of the pan leaves a clear channel for a few seconds. Season to taste with more salt, cayenne or chilli powder. Leave for 10 minutes, stir well, discard the ginger and then transfer to hot, dry sterilized jars (see page 8). Seal immediately, then invert (see page 10). Let cool before turning the right way up. Store for at least 1 month before using. After opening, keep covered in the refrigerator and use within 2 months.

cranberry & raisin chutney

A special homemade gift for Christmas or Thanksgiving, this chutney can be made at least a month in advance and it will keep for several months if stored in a cool, dark, dry place. It is the perfect accompaniment for Thanksgiving or Christmas turkey and ham, cheese and salads.

125 ml/½ cup white wine vinegar or cider vinegar

90 g/¾ cup raisins

90 g/¾ cup finely chopped nuts (Brazil nuts or almonds are best)

finely grated zest and freshly squeezed juice of 2 unwaxed lemons

½ teaspoon ground ginger

½ teaspoon paprika

½ teaspoon ground cinnamon

½ teaspoon salt

375 g/2 cups minus 2 tablespoons sugar

500 g/1 lb. 2 oz. fresh or frozen cranberries

Makes 1 litre/4 cups

Put all the ingredients, except the cranberries, into a preserving pan. Add 175 ml/¾ cup water, bring to the boil, reduce the heat and simmer until tender. Add the cranberries and simmer for 40 minutes or until the fruit is soft but not disintegrated, about 45 minutes.

Spoon into warm sterilized jars (see page 8). Cover and seal (see page 10). Store in a cool dark place for 2–3 weeks before using. After opening, keep covered in the refrigerator and use within 2 months.

apple jelly with lemon & fresh sage

Make this delicious jelly from windfall apples, if you are lucky enough to have access to them. If fresh sage is not available, mint makes a good alternative.

1.5 kg/3 lb. 5 oz. apples

warmed sugar (see page 10; for quantity see method)

freshly squeezed juice of 1 ½ lemons

a large bunch of fresh sage tied up tightly and leaving a long piece of string free

a few extra fresh sage leaves for decoration

a jelly bag or muslin/cheesecloth

Makes about 500 g/1 lb. 10 oz.

Peel, core and chop the apples. Put them in a preserving pan and add enough water, so that you can just see the water level appearing under the fruit. Part-cover with a lid and boil slowly until the fruit forms a pulp, 1–1 ½ hours.

Transfer the fruit pulp to a jelly bag suspended over a bowl. Leave to drip all night. (You can use a large piece of muslin/cheesecloth gathered into a bag and tied with string). Do not be tempted to squeeze the bag, as this will make the jelly cloudy.

Measure the juice obtained. Pour it into a large pan. Add 450 g/2¼ cups sugar for every 600 ml/2½ cups juice. Add the lemon juice. Set the pan over low heat and slowly dissolve the sugar, stirring all the while. When the sugar has dissolved, tie the bunch of sage to the handle of the pan and suspend in the jelly. Boil rapidly for 5–10 minutes until setting point is reached (see page 10). Stir from time to time to stop the pan burning.

When setting point has been reached, discard the sage and skim the jelly (see page 10). Stir the jelly and spoon into clean, dry, warm jars. Plunge a few fresh sage leaves into boiling water, pat dry and push one leaf into each jar. Seal (see page 10).

apricot chutney

This chutney can be made using either fresh or dried fruit. Here, the recipe uses fresh apricots, making the most of a seasonal glut. However, if you want to make it out of season, you can use dried apricots instead: simply replace the fresh apricots with 300 g/2 cups dried apricots, soaked for a few hours in the vinegar, then proceed in the same way.

1 teaspoon allspice

1 teaspoon mustard seeds

1 teaspoon ground coriander

1 small cinnamon stick

450 g/1 lb. fresh apricots, quartered and stoned/pitted

450 g/1 lb. cooking apples, peeled, cored and chopped into large chunks

750 ml/3¼ cups cider vinegar, wine vinegar or white malt vinegar

225 g/1½ cups sultanas/golden raisins, chopped

2 garlic cloves, peeled and chopped

zest and freshly squeezed juice of 1 unwaxed lemon

1 teaspoon salt

2-cm/¾-inch piece of fresh root ginger, peeled and finely chopped

450 g/2¼ cups warmed sugar (see page 10)

Makes 1.3 kg/3 lb.

Place the spices in a small piece of muslin/cheesecloth and tie it into a bag with string. Place the apricots, apples, vinegar and spice bag in a preserving pan and bring to the boil, then simmer for 10 minutes.

Add the other ingredients and stir over a low heat until all the sugar has dissolved, then bring to the boil and simmer for approximately 1½ hours until the chutney is thick but still juicy, stirring occasionally.

Remove the muslin/cheesecloth bag, then pour the chutney into hot, sterilized jars (see page 8) and seal (see page 10).

beetroot chutney

Beetroots/beets are another vegetable that at the height of the season you either have none of or far too many, so chutney-making suits them well. This recipes is delicious served with any soft, mild cheese, especially goat.

400 g/1 lb. raw beetroot/beet, peeled and coarsely grated

225 g/½ lb. onions, peeled and chopped

350 g/¾ lb. cooking apples, peeled, cored and chopped

225 g/1½ cups raisins

600 ml/2½ cups malt vinegar or spiced pickling vinegar (see page 12)

450 g/1 lb. sugar

1 teaspoon ground ginger

Makes about 1.3 kg /3 lb.

Place everything in a preserving pan and stir over a gentle heat to dissolve the sugar. Bring to the boil, then simmer gently for about 1 hour until the beetroot/beet and onions are soft and the chutney is thick but still juicy, stirring occasionally.

Pour the chutney into hot, sterilized jars (see page 8) and seal (see page 10).

damson chutney

This chutney is rich, dark and heavenly. Damsons are an excellent fruit for preserving and although removing the stones/pits is a laborious job, it is always worth the time since they lend a superb flavour across the board to any jam, jelly, chutney or pickle that uses them. Cook the fruits first, then remove the stones by hand.

1 kg/2 lb. 4 oz. damsons

1 litre/4 cups malt vinegar

1 cinnamon stick

1 tablespoon allspice

1 teaspoon cloves

300 g/10½ oz. cooking apples, peeled, cored and chopped

2 white onions, peeled and finely chopped

250 g/1¾ cups raisins

250 g/1¾ cups stoned/pitted dates, chopped

700 g/3½ cups soft brown sugar

2 garlic cloves, peeled and crushed

2 teapsoons ground ginger

1 tablespoon salt

Makes 2 kg/4 lb. 8 oz.

Place the damsons in a preserving pan with 250 ml/1 cup of the vinegar and cook them until they are soft and bursting. Leave until cool enough to handle, then remove the stones/pits. Place the spices in a small piece of muslin/cheesecloth and tie it into a bag with string.

Place all the ingredients in a preserving pan and bring to the boil, then simmer gently for 2–2½ hours until the chutney is dark and thick but still juicy, stirring from time to time.

Remove the muslin/cheesecloth bag, then pour the chutney into hot, sterilized jars (see page 8) and seal (see page 10).

green tomato & red onion chutney

1 kg/2 lb. 4 oz. green tomatoes

250 g/9 oz. cooking apples, peeled and cored

450 g/1 lb. red onions, roughly chopped

200 g/1 cup soft brown sugar

600 ml/2½ cups malt vinegar

½ teaspoon mustard seeds

½ teaspoon cayenne pepper

2-cm/1-inch piece of fresh root ginger, finely grated

200 g/7 oz. raisins

3 fresh green chillies/chiles, deseeded and finely chopped

1 teaspoon salt

Makes 1.75 kg/3 lb. 14 oz.

At the end of the season, when there is no more heat outside to ripen the last of the tomatoes, it is time to bring them into the house. If you place them on any empty windowsill you can find, there's a chance that the last precious fruits will slowly turn from green to red but if you have plenty to spare, the still-green ones are perfect for turning into this chutney.

To skin the tomatoes place them in a bowl and pour boiling water over them, then leave for a minute or two. The skins should now slide off the fruits when you cut into them with a sharp knife. It is harder to remove the skins when tomatoes are green, so steeping them for longer than usual helps. Chop the tomatoes roughly.

Place all the ingredients in a stainless steel preserving pan and bring to the boil. Reduce the heat and simmer for about 45 minutes to 1 hour until everything is cooked and the chutney has thickened, stirring occasionally.

Pour the chutney into hot, sterilized jars (see page 8) and seal (see page 10).

indian green mango chutney

1 white onion, cut into quarters

2–5 green and red fresh chillies/chiles (to taste), halved and deseeded

4-cm/2-inch piece of fresh ginger, peeled and cut into quarters

2 garlic cloves, peeled

1 tablespoon mixed mustard seeds

1 tablespoon cumin seeds

2 teaspoons ground turmeric

½ teaspoon salt

200 ml/¾ cup white wine vinegar

1 tablespoon olive oil

100 g/½ cup sugar

600 g/1 lb. 5 oz. green mangoes

Makes 800 ml/3 cups

This recipe, based on a traditional Indian pickle, goes well with spiced stir-fries and casseroles, roast meats and curries. Use hard green fruit since ripe fruits will disintegrate too much, and you want to retain texture.

Put the onion, chillies/chiles, ginger, garlic, mustard and cumin seeds, turmeric and salt in a blender, add 2–3 tablespoons of the vinegar and grind to a paste.

Put the oil in a saucepan and cook the paste over low heat for 10 minutes, adding the remaining vinegar as it cooks down. Add the sugar and continue cooking over low heat until dissolved.

Add the fruit to the pan, stir well and simmer until just tender but not soft, about 10 minutes. Spoon the chutney into warm sterilized jars (see page 8), cover and seal (see page 10).

coriander chutney

1 garlic clove, crushed

4 large, mild green fresh chillies/chiles, deseeded and chopped

3-cm/1¼-in piece of fresh ginger, peeled and chopped

a very large bunch of coriander/cilantro, leaves and stems chopped

1 teaspoon sugar

1 tablespoon freshly squeezed lemon or lime juice

1 tablespoon rapeseed (canola) oil

Makes about 125 ml/½ cup

Serve this traditional Indian fresh chutney with anything; it works well combined with yogurt and offered as a dip.

Put the garlic, chillies, ginger, coriander/cilantro and sugar in a small food processor or a large mortar and pestle and grind to a paste. While mixing, slowly add the lemon juice and oil. If necessary, mix in sufficient water to make a thick but spreadable paste.

The chutney is best eaten immediately, as it will quickly discolour. Store in an airtight container until ready to serve.

nectarine chutney

1 kg/2 lb. 4 oz. nectarines, skinned, stoned/pitted and roughly chopped

225 g/8 oz. cooking apples, peeled, cored and chopped

225 g/8 oz. white onions, peeled and thinly sliced

225 g/1½ cups raisins

350 g/1¾ cups light brown sugar

50 g/2 oz. stem ginger, finely chopped

2 garlic cloves

2 teaspoons salt

1 teaspoon cayenne pepper

500 ml/2 cups white wine vinegar

Makes 1.7 kg/3 lb. 12 oz.

Nectarines work so well here. They have just the right amount of sweetness and tartness to make an excellent chutney. Try this with macaroni cheese or put in a sandwich with just about anything!

Place all the ingredients in a preserving pan and stir over a gentle heat to dissolve the sugar. Simmer gently for approximately 1½ hours until the chutney is thick but still juicy, stirring occasionally.

Pour the chutney into hot, sterilized jars (see page 8) and seal (see page 10).

onion marmalade

Onion marmalade (really a chutney or relish, not a marmalade) at all has become very fashionable in recent years. Generally it isn't a great keeper but this particular recipe, like other cooked chutneys, will keep well.

1 kg/2 lb. 4 oz. red or white onions, peeled and finely sliced

2 tablespoons olive oil

500 ml/2 cups red wine vinegar (or a mixture of red vine vinegar and balsamic vinegar)

750 g/3 ¾ cups muscovado sugar

2 bay leaves

15–20 black peppercorns, crushed

2 teaspoons salt

Makes 1.25 kg/2 lb. 12 oz.

Separate the onion slices into rings. Heat the oil in a preserving pan, add the onion rings and cook them gently for about 20 minutes until they are soft but not browned.

Add all the other ingredients and simmer gently for 1–1½ hours until the marmalade is dark and thick but still juicy, stirring occasionally.

Pour the marmalade into hot, sterilized jars (see page 8) and seal (see page 10).

red tomato & garlic chutney

This is another easy classic that uses up a glut of summer tomatoes. Here, the red fruits and the brown sugar give the chutney a lovely rich colour.

1 teaspoon whole allspice

1 teaspoon coriander seeds

2 teaspoons mustard seeds

½ teaspoon cumin seeds

50-g/2-oz. piece of fresh root ginger, bruised

1.5 kg/3 lb. 5 oz. red tomatoes, skinned and chopped

500 g/1 lb. 2 oz. cooking apples, peeled, cored and diced

500 g/1 lb. 2 oz. white onions, peeled and finely chopped

2 garlic cloves, peeled and finely chopped

250 ml/1 cup red wine vinegar

1 teaspoon salt

200 g/1 cup warmed muscovado sugar (see page 10)

Makes 2 kg/4 lb. 8 oz.

Place the whole spices and bruised ginger in a piece of muslin/cheesecloth and tie it into a bag with string.

Place all the ingredients except the sugar in a stainless steel preserving pan and bring to the boil, then simmer until tender. Add the warmed sugar and stir over a low heat until all the sugar has dissolved. Turn up the heat and bring to the boil, then simmer gently for approximately 1½ hours until the chutney is thick but still juicy, stirring occasionally.

Remove the muslin/cheesecloth bag, then pour the chutney into hot, sterilized jars (see page 8) and seal (see page 10).

pumpkin chutney

With their wonderful shapes and textures pumpkins and other winter squashes are always so visually appealing and their flesh gives this chutney a colourful look and sweeter flavour – always a good thing.

12 peppercorns

2 teaspoons whole allspice

a 2-cm/¾-inch square piece of fresh root ginger, bruised

750 g/1 lb. 10 oz. pumpkin, peeled, deseeded and cut into chunks

450 g/1 lb. cooking apples, peeled, cored and finely chopped

50 g/2 oz. finely chopped stem ginger

350 g/12 oz. shallots, peeled, cored and finely chopped

200 g/1½ cups sultanas/golden raisins, chopped

2 garlic cloves, finely chopped

2 teaspoons salt

600 ml/2½ cups malt vinegar or cider vinegar

400 g/2 cups warmed soft brown sugar (see page 10)

Makes 2 kg/4 lb. 6 oz.

Place the dry spices and root ginger in a small piece of muslin/cheesecloth and tie it into a bag with string. Place all the ingredients except the sugar in a preserving pan and bring slowly to the boil, then simmer gently for 20 minutes until the pumpkin and apple are soft.

Add the warmed sugar and stir over a gentle heat until all the sugar has dissolved, then turn up the heat and simmer for approximately 1–1½ hours until the chutney is thick but still juicy, stirring occasionally.

Remove the muslin/cheesecloth bag, then pour the chutney into hot, sterilized jars (see page 8) and seal (see page 10).

pear chutney

This chutney contains just the right combination of fruitiness and spiciness. It is wise to let most chutney mature for a couple of months and this pear chutney is no exception, but it does taste remarkably good as soon as it is made.

1.3 kg/3 lbs. pears, peeled, cored and cut into chunks

450 g/1 lb. white onions, peeled and chopped

grated zest and freshly squeezed juice of 1 unwaxed lemon

grated zest and freshly squeezed juice of 1 unwaxed orange

225 g/1 cup plus 2 tablespoons sugar

225 g/1½ cups raisins

300 ml/1¼ cups malt vinegar or cider vinegar

1 teaspoon salt

1 teaspoon ground ginger

½ teaspoon whole cloves

Makes 1.7 kg/3 lb. 12 oz.

Place all the ingredients in a preserving pan and stir over a gentle heat until all the sugar has dissolved. Bring to the boil, then simmer for approximately 2 hours until the chutney is dark and thick but still juicy, stirring occasionally. As with all chutneys, it will thicken up slightly as it cools.

Pour the chutney into hot, sterilized jars (see page 8) and seal (see page 10).

You'll find these easy recipes are a delicious way to liven up even the simplest of dishes, from grilled fish and cold meats, to cheese plates. They also make welcome homemade gifts during the festive season.

pickles & relishes

layered pickled vegetables

This attractive pickle is easy to prepare. It is tempting to keep it on show, but like most preserves it is best kept in the dark. Serve as part of an Italian-style antipasti with olives, cheese and cold meats.

1 large yellow (bell) pepper

1 large red (bell) pepper

1 large orange (bell) pepper

2 young tender carrots

4 small courgettes/zucchini

1 celery heart

1 garlic clove

1 fresh red or green chilli/chile

a sprig of fresh dill or oregano

salt

For the brine mix:

1 tablespoon salt

75 ml/⅓ cup white wine vinegar

2 teaspoons sugar

2 clean, dry, warm jars with lids, 500 ml/2 cups capacity each. Choose jars that are tall and thin rather than short and wide

Makes 1 litre/4 cups

Wash or wipe all the vegetables thoroughly. Deseed the peppers and slice into rings. Cut the carrots, courgettes/zucchini and celery into strips. Layer the vegetables in a colander set over a bowl, sprinkling salt on each layer. Put a weighted plate on top and let stand overnight covered with a cloth.

To make the brine, put 300 ml/1¼ cups water in a saucepan, add the salt, vinegar, garlic and sugar. Bring gently to the boil, then remove from the heat, cover and let cool.

The following morning, put the vegetables in a colander and pour boiling water over them. Drain and dry thoroughly with a clean cloth. Pack them into the jars in layers, starting with half the red pepper rings, half the celery, followed by half the orange pepper, half the courgettes/zucchini, half the yellow pepper rings and finishing with the remaining celery and half the carrot. Top up each layer of vegetables with brine as you go. When the jar is full, insert the garlic, chilli/chile and dill.

Top up the jars to the brim with brine. Tap the sides of the jars to bring any air bubbles to the surface or slide a thin knife blade down the inside of the jars to release them. Seal and leave for at least 1 week before using. Store for 6–12 months. After opening, the flavour of the pickles starts to deteriorate, so finish them straight away.

sweet & sour pickled onions

Pickled onions and gherkins are traditional accompaniments to pâtés and terrines, helping to cut through the richness and, in some cases, the fattiness of these dishes. They are also perfect served with a strong, mature cheese.

500 g/1 lb. 2 oz. pickling onions
(if not in season, use shallots)

25 g/1 oz. salt

1 cinnamon stick

3 small fresh hot red chillies/chiles

2 teaspoons black peppercorns

85 g/½ cup raisins

200 g/1 cup sugar

375 ml/1½ cups white wine vinegar

125 ml/½ cup Moscatel or sherry vinegar

Makes about 1 litre/4 cups

Trim the tops and bottoms off the onions, keeping enough flesh to hold the onions together. Bring a large saucepan of water to the boil and remove from the heat. Put the onions in the water and leave them to sit for 1 minute, then drain.

Have a bowl of iced water ready. Peel the skins off the onions, discard and drop the onions straight into the water. When they are all peeled, drain them and put them in a bowl. Sprinkle with the salt to coat. Cover with a dish towel and leave overnight.

The next day, rinse the onions, dry them on paper towels and transfer to a sterilized jar.

Put the cinnamon, chillies/chiles, peppercorns, raisins, sugar, vinegar and Moscatel in a saucepan and bring to the boil, stirring until the sugar has dissolved. Pour the hot liquid with its spices over the onions. Seal (see page 10) and store for at least 2 weeks before serving. Eat within 6 months.

lemons in olive oil

6 large unwaxed lemons, washed and thinly sliced

3 tablespoons salt

1½ teaspoons paprika, preferably Spanish pimentón

2 small dried red chillies (optional)

2–4 small fresh bay leaves

up to 750 ml/3 cups mild olive oil (not extra virgin) or half sunflower and half mild olive oil

Makes 2 x 500 ml/2 cup jars

Here salted lemon slices are covered with olive oil and paprika for a mellow, amber-coloured preserve. Alternatively, you can preserve whole lemons in salt and lemon juice for a sharp and tangy flavour (see method below).

Lay the lemon slices on trays in a single layer and sprinkle the salt over them, then freeze overnight. The following day, let them thaw and drain off the juices. Dab dry with paper towels.

Layer the lemon slices in 2 sterilized jars, sprinkling a little paprika between the layers. Add a chilli to each jar, if using, and tuck in 1–2 bay leaves. Cover to at least 1 cm/¼ inch depth with oil. Leave for 30 minutes, then tap several times on the work surface to dispel any air bubbles. Cover then seal tightly.

lemons in sea salt

14–15 small, fine-skinned unwaxed lemons, washed, plus extra freshly squeezed lemon juice as necessary

90 g/3¼ oz. sea salt, plus 2 tablespoons

1 tablespoon sugar

Makes a 1 kg/2 lb. 4 oz. jar

Pack as many lemons into a 1 kg/2 lb. 4 oz. jar as you can. Take them out, put them in a bowl with the 2 tablespoons salt and pour cold water over to cover. Keep the lemons submerged with a plate and leave for 24 hours.

Make two deep lengthways cuts into each soaked lemon and pack 1 teaspoon salt into each lemon. Sterilize the jar, then sprinkle a thin layer of salt on the base. Pack in the lemons, sprinkling in the remaining salt and sugar as you go. Press the lemons down hard. Squeeze the juice from the remaining lemons and strain it over the lemons in the jar to cover. Cover then seal tightly. Leave for 1 week in a cool, dark spot, shaking the jar every day.

Both recipes should be stored in a dark, cool place for at least 4 weeks before using.

spiced pickled cherries

Pickled cherries have long been a popular match for French charcuterie, going especially well with pork and duck. You can use sweet or sour cherries, leaving the stalks on for an elegant finish if liked.

450 g/2¼ cups sugar

500 ml/2 cups white wine vinegar

2 teaspoons black peppercorns

6 cloves

2 star anise

1 cinnamon stick

500 g/1 lb. 2 oz. sweet or sour fresh cherries, rinsed

Makes about 1 litre/4 cups

Put the sugar, vinegar, peppercorns, cloves, star anise and cinnamon in a saucepan and heat, stirring until the sugar has dissolved. Reduce the heat to a simmer and cook for 8 minutes. Leave to cool.

Sort through the cherries, discarding any that are bruised or split. Pack them into a sterilized jar and pour over the cold liquid with its spices. Seal and store for a few weeks before eating. The cherries will keep for up to 1 year.

red cabbage & currant pickle

3 tablespoons olive oil

½ small red cabbage, thinly sliced

60 ml/¼ cup red wine

3 tablespoons brown sugar

60 ml/¼ cup balsamic vinegar

35 g/¼ cup currants

35 g/¼ cup pine nuts

Makes about 500 ml/2 cups

This instant sweet-and-sour pickle is great served with rich meats such as sausages or game.

Heat the oil in a large frying pan/skillet set over low to medium heat. Add the cabbage, cover and cook for 5 minutes. Turn up the heat to high, add the wine and let it bubble, then add the sugar, vinegar and currants. Cook, stirring, for 5 minutes.

Heat a separate small frying pan skillet, add the pine nuts and toast, stirring, until golden. Stir the toasted pine nuts into the pickle. Let cool and refrigerate until needed. The pickle will keep in the refrigerator for up to 2 weeks.

crisp apple & ginger pickle

½ teaspoon fenugreek seeds

½ teaspoon black mustard seeds

½ teaspoon turmeric

½ teaspoon salt

1 tablespoon crushed chilli paste

1 tablespoon mustard oil or plain-flavoured oil, such as grapeseed

2 green apples, cored and cut into 2-cm/¾-inch pieces

5-cm/2-inch piece of fresh ginger, peeled and grated

70 g/½ cup raisins

Makes about 500 ml/2 cups

Serving a very hot, fresh pickle is a great way to let people add more heat if they like it. Raisins add a sweetness that complements the spice. This is especially good with pork, sausages, chicken and roasted root vegetables.

Heat a frying pan/skillet over medium heat and add the fenugreek and mustard seeds. Cook, stirring constantly, for about 1 minute, until fragrant. Transfer to a mortar and pestle with the turmeric and salt and grind together. Add the chilli paste and oil and pound to make a paste.

Put the apple pieces, ginger and raisins, if using, in a bowl and stir in the paste until well combined. Cover and refrigerate until needed. The pickle will keep in the refrigerator for up to 2 days.

300 g/10½ oz. watermelon rind

100 ml/⅓ cup white vinegar

150 g/¾ cup sugar

5 whole cloves

1-cm/½-inch piece of cinnamon stick

1-cm/½-inch piece of fresh ginger, crushed

a fluted or frilled pastry wheel

Makes 375 g/13 oz.

sweet watermelon rind pickle

This old Virginian recipe turns hefty wedges of peel left after a feast of watermelon into something delicious. The finished pickle is a lovely, soft, dark green and you may be surprised how much flavour watermelon rind has. Eat it with any cured, boiled or baked ham and try it with cheese.

Using the pastry wheel, cut the rind into tiny squares. Put in a bowl, add the white vinegar and 100 ml/⅛ cup water, cover and let stand overnight.

Next morning, put the pieces of rind in a sieve and let drain for 2 hours or until quite dry. Discard the liquid. Transfer the fruit rind to a piece of paper towel to absorb any remaining moisture.

To make the syrup, put the sugar and 350 ml/1½ cups water in a saucepan. Put the cloves, cinnamon and ginger in a spice ball or tie in a muslin bag and attach it to the handle of the pan so the spices are suspended in the syrup. Heat slowly to simmering point to dissolve the sugar, then boil for 10 minutes. Add the melon rind and simmer for 3 minutes.

Scoop out the rind with a slotted spoon and put in the jar. Keep boiling the syrup until it has thickened, then pour it over the rind to fill the jar. Seal the jar at once then let cool.

Store in a dark cupboard for 1 month before tasting – invert the jar from time to time to make sure the sugar does not crystallize on the bottom.

pickled chillies

about 750 g/1½ lb. red serrano chillies/chiles, each one about 5 cm/2 inches long

250 ml/1 cup white wine vinegar

200 g/1 cup caster/superfine sugar

½ teaspoon salt

Makes about 1 litre/4 cups

These chillies are so decorative that it's tempting to have a jar on show in the kitchen, even if you never open it!

Thoroughly wash and drain the chillies/chiles. Leave them whole or halve them lengthways and remove the seeds if you prefer.

Put them in a saucepan with the vinegar, sugar and salt. Bring to the boil and let simmer until the sugar has dissolved and the chillies are tender, about 6–8 minutes.

Remove from the heat and let cool before packing into the jars. Seal tightly then store in the refrigerator. Leave for 2 weeks before using. After opening, keep covered in the refrigerator and use within 2–3 weeks.

Note: When handling chillies, wear gloves, or use tongs or a knife and fork, and keep your hands well away from your eyes.

preserved sweet chillies

125 g/4½ oz. medium to large fresh red chillies/chiles

450 g/2¼ cups sugar

450 ml/1¾ cups white wine vinegar

Makes 500 ml/2 cups

The perfect gift for friends who enjoy hot and spicy food.

Slice the chillies/chiles crossways into 2-cm/1-inch pieces. Rinse well and drain, removing as many seeds as possible for a less fiery flavour. Put the chillies and sugar into a heavy-based saucepan and add the vinegar. Bring slowly to the boil, then let simmer until the chillies are tender, about 5–7 minutes. Remove from the heat and set aside to cool. Spoon into jars and seal.

Store in a cool, dark place for 2 weeks before using. After opening, keep covered in the refrigerator and use within 2–3 weeks.

tomato, lemon & courgette relish

Pickled or preserved lemons develop such a unique and wonderful flavour that is captured in this tomato and courgette relish. It makes a great accompaniment to sausages, lamb, chicken and hard cheeses.

2 small unwaxed lemons

500 g/1 lb. 2 oz. courgettes/zucchini, finely chopped

2 red or white onions, finely chopped

4 tablespoons salt

1 kg/2 lb. 4 oz. tomatoes, chopped

150 g/¾ cup sugar

375 ml/1½ cups white wine vinegar or cider vinegar

1 tablespoon white mustard seeds

1 teaspoon dill seeds or celery seeds

¼ teaspoon turmeric

Makes about 1.2 litres/5 cups

Carefully cut the rind from the lemons, with a very thin layer of white pith. Finely chop and put in a glass or ceramic bowl with the juice from 1 of the lemons. Put the courgettes/zucchini and onions in separate bowls. Sprinkle each with the salt, cover and leave at room temperature overnight. When ready to make the relish, rinse well with cold water and drain thoroughly.

Put the tomatoes, sugar and vinegar in a large saucepan and bring to the boil, stirring constantly to dissolve the sugar. Reduce to a simmer and cook for 1 hour, stirring occasionally, until thick. Bring back to the boil and add the drained lemon rind, courgettes/zucchini and onions with the mustard seeds, dill seeds and turmeric. Cook for 5 minutes. Spoon into sterilized jars and seal (see page 10). The relish will keep for up to 1 year if sealed correctly.

crunchy sweetcorn & pepper relish

3 (bell) peppers, 1 red, 1 yellow and 1 orange

sweetcorn kernels from 2 corn-on-the-cobs

1 red or white onion, chopped

4 tablespoons salt

1 teaspoon white mustard seeds

½ teaspoon cumin seeds

½ teaspoon coriander seeds

½ teaspoon whole black peppercorns

6 small dried red chillies/chiles

375 ml/1½ cups white vinegar

115 g/½ cup plus 1 tablespoon sugar

¼ teaspoon turmeric

Makes about 900 ml/4 cups

Fresh sweetcorn and colourful peppers make such a vibrant relish and the crunchy texture also adds appeal. You can serve the relish the day you make it, but it's even better preserved and stored.

Remove the stems from the peppers and discard. Cut the peppers into 2-cm/¾-in dice and put in a colander with the sweetcorn and onion. Toss with the salt and leave for 2–4 hours. Rinse well with cold water and shake dry.

Heat a saucepan over medium heat and add the mustard, cumin and coriander seeds, peppercorns and chillies. Cook, stirring, for 1 minute until fragrant. Add the vinegar, sugar and turmeric and bring to the boil, stirring to dissolve the sugar.

Add the rinsed sweetcorn, peppers and onion to the vinegar mixture. Cover and bring to the boil.

If using immediately, let cool, stirring occasionally. To preserve, fill sterilized jars (see page 8) with the relish while it is still hot and seal (see page 10). The relish will keep for up to 2 months if sealed correctly.

cranberry & pear relish

300 g/3 heaped cups fresh cranberries

200 g/1 cup demerara sugar

1 cinnamon stick

1 teaspoon ground ginger

grated zest and freshly squeezed juice of 1 unwaxed orange

4 ripe pears

Makes about 600 g/1 lb. 4 oz.

This is the perfect winter relish, as it goes well with baked ham or roast turkey. Why not tie the jars up with labels and ribbons and give away as gifts?

Put the cranberries, 150 ml/⅔ cup water, the sugar, cinnamon stick, ground ginger and orange zest and juice into a preserving pan. Cook until the cranberries have softened and burst, then simmer for another 5 minutes.

Peel the pears, cut into quarters and remove the cores. Chop the pears into small pieces and add to the pan. Cook for a further 15–20 minutes until the pears are soft and the sauce has thickened.

Remove the pan from the heat. Remove the cinnamon stick. Taste the sauce and add a little more sugar if needed.

Spoon the relish into sterilized jars (see page 10), leave to cool, then seal. Store in the refrigerator for up to 2 weeks.

fig relish

125 g/1 cup ready-to-eat dried figs, roughly chopped

50 g/⅓ cup pitted/stoned dates, roughly chopped

1 shallot, sliced

1 small eating apple, peeled, cored and finely diced

2 tablespoons light muscovado sugar

125 ml/½ cup white wine vinegar or cider vinegar

1 teaspoon grated orange zest

1 cinnamon stick

1 fresh or dried bay leaf

Makes 6 servings

This simply-to-make yet delicious fig relish is perfect served with a chicken liver paté or duck parfait.

Tip all the ingredients into a saucepan. Cook over low heat for about 25 minutes, or until tender and jammy.

Remove the cinnamon stick and bay leaf, season and let cool before serving. Store, covered, in the refrigerator for up to 2 weeks.

roasted pear relish

4 ripe pears, peeled, halved and cored

2 tablespoons freshly squeezed lemon juice

1 tablespoon light brown sugar

50 g/1¾ oz. white sugar

¾ teaspoon ground cinnamon

¼ teaspoon ground cloves

65 ml/¼ cup pure maple syrup

1 small red onion, sliced

1 tablespoon grated fresh ginger

5 tablespoons raisins

125 ml/½ cup cider vinegar

1 teaspoon dried red chilli/hot pepper flakes (optional)

vegetable oil, for brushing

Makes 6 servings

A fantastic accompaniment to roast pork and poultry.

Preheat the oven to 180°C (350°F) Gas 4. Brush a baking sheet with oil. Combine the pears, lemon juice, both the sugars, cinnamon and cloves in a bowl and mix well. Arrange the pears cut-side down on the baking sheet and brush with oil. Roast in the preheated oven for about 45 minutes, until caramelized. When cool enough to handle, cut into small cubes.

Meanwhile, put the remaining ingredients in a preserving pan and bring to the boil. Reduce the heat and simmer, uncovered, for 5 minutes. Remove from the heat and let cool. Add the pears and mix well. Cover and refrigerate for at least 1 day. Transfer to a spotlessly clean and dry, sealable airtight container. The relish will keep in the refrigerator for up to 10 days.

cranberry & basil relish

This jewel-bright relish is delicious served with your thanksgiving or Christmas turkey and a rich, fruity aroma fills the house when it's cooking. It also works well in sandwiches with cold turkey and ham, or simply alongside some mature cheeses.

2 tablespoons light olive oil

1 red onion, finely chopped

2 garlic cloves, crushed

350 g/3½ heaped cups fresh or frozen cranberries (no need to thaw)

100 g/½ cup demerara sugar

50 ml/¼ cup less 1 tablespoon red wine vinegar

leaves from a small bunch of fresh basil

¼ teaspoon salt

freshly ground black pepper

Makes 400 ml/14 fl. oz.

Heat the oil in a large, heavy frying pan/skillet, preferably non-stick. Add the onion and garlic and cook gently, stirring occasionally, for 5 minutes.

Add the rest of the ingredients to the pan and stir well. Cook over medium heat, stirring frequently, until very thick, about 10 minutes.

Taste and adjust the seasoning, adding more salt or a few grinds of pepper as needed. Spoon into the sterilized jars (see page 8) and seal (see page 10). When completely cold, store in the refrigerator and use within 1 month.

ginger fruit relish

5 unwaxed oranges

2 pears

2 green apples, fairly tart

90 ml/⅓ cup white wine vinegar

200 g/1 cup light muscovado sugar

a 5-cm/2-inch piece of fresh ginger, peeled and grated

1 teaspoon salt

50 g/⅓ cup raisins

grated zest and freshly squeezed juice of 1 unwaxed lemon

Makes about 800 ml/3½ cups

A zingy relish that can be made at any time of the year, however it is particularly good with cold ham and cheese, so it makes an excellent gift during the festive season.

Rinse the oranges, then grate the zest and reserve. Using a serrated knife, peel the oranges to remove all the skin and the white pith. Cut into small chunks, discarding the pips.

Peel and core the pears and apples, and cut into chunks the same size as the oranges.

Put the vinegar and sugar into a preserving pan and heat gently, stirring frequently to dissolve the sugar.

Add the grated ginger and salt to the pan. Bring to the boil, then stir in the chopped fruit. Boil gently for 20 minutes, stirring frequently until the fruit is very soft.

Stir in the reserved orange rind, the raisins and the grated lemon zest and juice.

Cook for another 10–15 minutes, stirring frequently, until very thick and no longer watery on top.

Remove the pan from the heat and stir well. Spoon into the sterilized jars (see page 8) and seal (see page 10). Leave to cool, then store for up to 1 month. Once opened, keep in the refrigerator for up to 2 weeks.

index

picture credits

Steve Baxter
Pages 75, 130 bkgrd, 136,
138 bkgrd

Martin Brigdale
Pages 3, 48, 91 insert, 128,
138 insert

Peter Cassidy
Pages 1, 11 insert, 30 bkgrd,
31, 38–39, 64, 82, 83, 89, 90,
91 bkgrd, 96 bkgrd, 119, 122
insert, 123–125, 131, 132

Laura Edwards
Page 45

Tara Fisher
Pages 17, 40, 44, 47, 61, 65, 85,
86, 93, 102, 115, 116, 117 insert,
118 insert, 127

Jonathan Gregson
Pages 4–5, 14, 56

Winfried Heinze
Pages 23 insert

Caroline Hughes
Page 7

Richard Jung
Pages 25, 52, 57, 58, 72 insert, 74,
88 insert, 92 insert, 120, 130 insert

Lisa Linder
Pages 6, 29 bkgrd, 53 bkgrd,
95 bkgrd, 108 bkgrd, 129, 134,
135, 142–145

William Lingwood
Pages 78–79 bkgrd

Mark Lohman
Page 84 insert

Emma Mitchell
Page 78

Gloria Nicol
Pages 2, 8 all inserts b, 13 insert,
16 insert, 18 and 19 insert, 21
insert, 22 insert, 24, 25 insert, 26
insert, 27, 28, 29 insert, 30 insert,
32, 33 insert, 34 insert, 35 insert,
46 insert, 49 insert, 51, 54 insert,
55, 59 insert, 63 insert, 66, 68
insert, 69, 70, 73 insert, 77, 79
insert, 80, 94, 95 insert, 96 insert,
97, 98, 99 insert, 100 insert, 101,
105, 106, 107 insert, 108 insert,
109, 110, 111 insert, 112 insert,
113

Steve Painter
Pages 12–13 bkgrd, 42, 76 bkgrd,
107 bkgrd, 122 bkgrd

William Reavell
Pages 10–11 bkgrd, 15, 26 bkgrd,
37, 43, 49 bkgrd, 54 bkgrd, 59
bkgrd, 92 bkgrd, 114, 118 bkgrd,
139, 140

Claire Richardson
Page 81

Lucinda Symons
Page 62

Debi Treloar
Pages 20, 60 insert

Kate Whitaker
Pages 4–5 bkgrd, 8–9 bkgrd, 16
bkgrd, 21–23 bkgrd, 33–35 bkgrd,
48 bkgrd, 36, 41, 50, 60 bkgrd,
63 bkgrd, 67, 68 bkgrd, 71, 72–73
bkgrd, 76 insert, 84 bkgrd, 87, 88
bkgrd, 99 bkgrd, 100 bkgrd, 103,
104, 111 bkgrd, 112 bkgrd, 117
bkgrd, 121, 126, 133, 137, 141

recipe credits

Gloria Nicol
Jam-making basics 6–13
Apple and blackcurrant marmalade
Apricot chutney
Apricot curd
Apricot jam
Beetroot chutney
Bitter orange curd
Blackcurrant jelly
Blueberry and lime curd
Cherry jam
Damson chutney
Green fig jam
Green tomato and red onion
    chutney
Green tomato jam
Lemon and fig marmalade
Nectarine chutney
Onion marmalade
Peach and pear jam
Peach and raspberry jam
Peach marmalade
Pear and vanilla jam
Pear chutney
Plum jam
Pumpkin chutney
Quince and orange marmalade
Raspberry curd
Raspberry jam
Red tomato and garlic chutney
Seville orange marmalade
Strawberry and gooseberry jam
Strawberry and vanilla jam
Tutti fruitti jam
White currant and red chilli jam

Lindy Wildsmith
Apple jelly with lemon and sage
Chunky lemon, lime and grapefruit
    marmalade
Dried apricot conserve
Grannie's apple chutney
Indian green mango chutney
Italian fig conserve
Layered pickled vegetables
Orange and kumquat marmalade
Pineapple and apple jam
Pumpkin and red tomato chutney
Williamsburg sweet watermelon
    rind pickle

Laura Washburn
Apple blackberry jam
Apple butter
Apple pumpkin jam
Apple red onion and dried cherry
    chutney
Apple, pear and ginger chutney
Roasted pear relish

Fiona Smith
Coriander chutney
Crisp apple and ginger pickle
Crunchy sweetcorn and pepper
    relish
Red cabbage and currant pickle
Spiced pickled cherries
Sweet and sour pickled onions
Tomato, lemon and courgette/
    zucchini relish

Linda Collister
Cranberry and basil relish
Ginger fruit relish
Maple squash butter
Red fruit conserve

Kay Fairfax
Cranberry and raisin chutney
Grapefruit and lime curd
Pickled chillies
Preserved sweet chillies

Brian Glover
Lemon curd
Lemons in olive oil
Lemons in sea salt
Squash and aubergine chutney

Tonia George
Peppermint tea and apple jelly
White tea and apricot jam

Annie Rigg
Cranberry and pear relish
Fig relish

Liz Franklin
Easy chilli jam